The Book of David

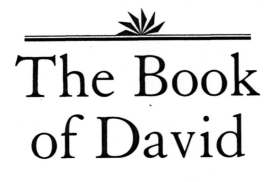

The Book of David

of David

*How Preserving Families
Can Cost Children's Lives*

RICHARD J. GELLES

BASIC
BOOKS

A Member of the Perseus Books Group

Designed by Elliott Beard

Library of Congress Cataloging-in-Publication Data
    Gelles, Richard J.
    The book of David: how perserving families can cost
children's lives / Richard J. Gelles.
        p.   cm.
    Includes bibliographical references and index.
    ISBN 0-465-05395-5 (cloth)
    ISBN 0-465-05396-3 (paper)
    1. Child abuse—United States—Prevention.
2. Child welfare—United States. 3. Family violence—
United States—Prevention.
    I. Title.
    HV6626.52.G44   1996   95-34242
    362.7'67'0973—dc20   CIP

        99 00 ◆/RRD 9 8 7 6 5 4 3

To my wife, Judy

Contents

Preface

I CAN STILL SEE THE AUTOPSY SLIDE OF A LITTLE BOY I CALL
David Edwards. He was not grossly disfigured like the battered
children in the pictures typically displayed to professionals
and the public. In fact, David looked like he was asleep on a
white sheet. But he was dead, suffocated by his mother. What
haunts me about David is that we know enough about child
abuse that we could have, and should have, saved his life. I
cannot bear to see many more such pictures. I cannot bear to
be involved in more fatality reviews of little babies. I cannot
bear the frustration of devoting a lifetime of research and
practice to the ideal of protecting children only to find that
current policies ignore the research results. We must change
the system. We will change the system.

I chose to focus on Marie and David Edwards (pseudonyms) in this book because they provide a clear and vivid window into how the system operates. The chronology and basic facts of David's life and death and the abuse of his older sister come from a public report of the investigation into David's death. The dates in this book conform to the chronology of the report. I have, however, altered some of the details in order to protect the privacy of all the individuals involved. To do this, I have incorporated facts from other child fatalities. Some background information on parents and grandparents has been changed, as have biographical and case descriptions of the clinicians involved. Thus, although I follow the outline of Marie and David's case, this is a composite case.

Acknowledgments

I HAVE BEEN FORTUNATE TO WORK WITH MANY TALENTED and generous friends and colleagues in the course of my career and over the five years that I have worked on this book. First, I would like to acknowledge the members of the University of Rhode Island Family Violence Research Program. Glenn Wolfner, Jody Brown, Deborah Levesque, Heidi Reckseik, Jan O'Kelley, Lisa Zamara, Joseph Youngblood, and Chris Ferland provided assistance and much-needed emotional support.

I have also been fortunate to have colleagues around the country who listened to my argument and offered helpful suggestions and pointed criticism. Murray Straus, Eli and Carolyn Newberger, Tom Curran, Lucy Berliner, Peter Hellman, Cassie Beven, Mark Patinkin, and Stuart Hart provided general encouragement and specific suggestions along the way. Of course, they are not responsible for, nor have they endorsed, any of the specific opinions or proposals I present in the book.

I owe a special debt to two friends and colleagues who played a major role in shaping my ideas and motivating me to undertake this book. Laureen D'Ambra, the Rhode Island Child Advocate, introduced me to the most disturbing facet of child abuse and neglect: the process of investigating child fatalities. Laureen taught me the value of trying to learn from these terrible events and to use that knowledge to improve the system. John Symynkywicz, the president of Dawn for Children, a child advocacy group in Rhode Island, not only was my role model for being a child advocate, but dragged me kicking and screaming out of the ivory tower into the daily, shirt-sleeve world of grassroots child advocacy.

Partial funding for the research that led to this book came from the Harry Frank Guggenheim Foundation. I am grateful to Karen Colvard, program officer for the foundation, for her support and assistance.

Jo Ann Miller has been an absolutely wonderful editor. First, she believed in the book; second, she helped me shape and focus the presentation. Her comments and criticisms were right on target and I am in her debt. Many thanks to Anne Montague, who transformed my academic prose into a readable book.

My wife, Judy, to whom this book is dedicated, and my sons, Jason and David, are patient and caring sources of support. Without their love and warmth, I could never have been able to stay for a quarter of a century with a topic as dark and grim as child abuse.

It may not be a fixed rule but it is certainly a convention of public tragedy that it must repeat itself if it is to make a cry loud enough for something good to come of it.

—Norman Maclean, *Young Men and Fire*

The Book of David

I

A Dangerous World

ON A BRISK AUTUMN MORNING IN 1990 A FIRE RESCUE UNIT
pulled in front of two parked cars and came to an abrupt stop
at the emergency ambulance entrance of Providence Hospital.
The driver, an emergency medical technician (EMT), quickly
walked to the rear of the ambulance and, along with her part-
ner in back, pulled the stretcher from the van. The figure under
the sheet was so small it seemed but a bump of rumpled clothing in the middle of the stretcher. Fifteen-month-old David
Edwards was that bump. A small round oxygen mask attached
to an inflatable bag covered most of his ashen-bluish face. Thin
strands of blond hair stuck out from under the mask.

David was unconscious. The rescue team had been called to
the Edwards home at 7:45 A.M. by Darlene Edwards, who told

the 911 operator that her son wasn't breathing. When the team arrived, they ran up the stairs to the Edwardses' second-floor apartment. Darlene was with David in his bedroom, a typical baby's room with newly painted walls, a crib, changing table, and boxes of diapers stacked in the corner. Baby clothes were neatly folded on the bureau next to the changing table, and assorted toys were in the crib and around the room.

Twenty-three-year-old Darlene Edwards leaned over the crib railing and stared at her immobile child. She made no move to hold him, comfort him, or help him. She simply stared. An EMT picked the boy up, checked for his breathing and pulse, and immediately began cardiopulmonary resuscitation (CPR).

CPR of an unconscious baby is a harsh and invasive procedure. A curved, rigid breathing tube was inserted into David's mouth to open his airway; the gentle force necessary to place the tube dislodged two front teeth and opened a bloody gash in the mouth. The EMTs began external cardiac compressions in hopes of moving oxygenated blood from David's non-functioning heart to the brain. Despite the proper procedure of pressing his chest five times for every breath, with just enough pressure to accomplish this task, two cracks were soon heard, one for each of two broken ribs. Initial attempts to insert an intravenous line (IV) failed. Three minutes after arriving, an EMT placed David on his left forearm and continued CPR while carrying him to the back of the ambulance, where he placed him on a stretcher and hooked him up to a cardiac monitor. But nothing beyond continuing CPR could be done during the five-minute ride to the hospital.

David's body temperature was 90 degrees when he was admitted to the emergency room. His lack of blood pressure made it impossible to insert the IV. Cardiac massage and the injection of epinephrine failed to stimulate any cardiac response. At 8:42 A.M. David Edwards was pronounced dead. The provisional cause of death listed was cardiac arrest.

After David's body was transported to the office of the state medical examiner, Peter Delaney, the emergency room physician who had treated him, placed a call to the Child Abuse and Neglect Tracking System (CANTS) hotline of the Department of Children and Their Families. Because he could not be sure of what exactly had caused David's heart to fail, the physician followed the legal mandate to report all suspicious deaths to the hotline.

At the office of the state medical examiner, David's lifeless body gave few clues to the cause of death. There was considerable dried blood around his mouth, but that was the result of the breathing tube insertion. David also had numerous other marks on his body: scrapes behind both ears, twelve small bruises on his back, one or two bruises on his buttocks, and a mysterious diamond-shaped cluster of pinprick marks on his thigh. Some of the bruises might have been caused by the CPR, but others were in different stages of healing, and therefore of differing ages, and had clearly occurred prior to the morning of his death.

An internal examination revealed a number of telling facts. First, his lungs were "hyperinflated"; the boy had taken in air but had been unable to expel it. Some force had compressed the boy's diaphragm—possibly from his being wedged between a mattress and crib rails or from being held face-down on a mattress. There were also small hemorrhages in David's eyes, face, and lungs, suggestive of asphyxiation. Finally, his colon contained a large, hard feces, which in a fifteen-month-old would be a sure sign that the baby was colicky and cranky.

Department of Children and Their Families policy requires a response within ten minutes by a child protection investigator to a reported death of a child. A three-pronged investigation of David Edwards's death was under way by noon on October 16 while the medical examiner continued conducting an autopsy. Investigator Ron Hassey first checked the CANTS computerized records to determine whether David or his family had prior contact with either CANTS or the department. What he found was distressing. The family had indeed had contact with both CANTS and the department; in fact, David had been an "open" case of suspected child neglect since shortly after his birth. A caseworker in the department's assessment unit had closed David Edwards's case less than three months earlier. She had not found what she or the department's attorneys considered compelling evidence that David was a victim of abuse or neglect. An anonymous caller had alleged that he had a chipped elbow, but the medical report did not offer enough evidence to establish that the injury had been inflicted by the parents. The X-ray provided by the hospital was of the uninjured elbow. No one in the CANTS unit had bothered to obtain the X-ray of the supposed injured arm. A second report that David was not gaining weight and might be a "failure to thrive" baby was not supported with evidence. A neighbor's complaint that the parents were using marijuana, because the hallway smelled of it, was not given much attention by the caseworker. Although the caseworker made no mention in the case record of her feelings about the parents, she had told her supervisor that she was afraid of Donald and Darlene Edwards. As we will see, David's father was enraged that the Department of Children and Their Families had removed his daughter, Marie, from the home after she had been severely injured, and he had vowed he would never let the department take his son away. He ranted at the caseworker each time she visited to investigate a report that David was being abused and neglected.

Investigator Hassey began with the emergency room physician's report of the suspicious death. He would soon get a copy of the full "Physician's Report of Examination," which provided more details on the case. Hassey left his desk on the CANTS call floor and went to the Edwards home, where he interviewed Darlene and Donald Edwards.

Postmortem investigations are delicate affairs. Hassey did not want to accuse the parents directly of wrongdoing, since there was a chance that David had died from accidental suffocation or even sudden infant death syndrome (SIDS). Hassey began with general questions about David's health and sleeping habits and gradually turned his questioning to the bruises on David' body. Both parents immediately denied any responsibility. They said David often bruised himself when he fell on his toys. They reported that they had been the only caretakers for David for the week preceding the 911 call and that David had slept from 8:30 P.M. to 5:30 A.M. on the morning of his death. Neither parent could explain why their son had stopped breathing some time between 5:30 and 7:45. The parents displayed no sign of grief or other emotion during Hassey's interview, and most of their answers were delivered in a flat monotone.

The police were the second prong of the three-pronged investigation. First, they went to the home, retrieved the crib, mattress, and bedding, and delivered them to the medical examiner. The medical examiner, the third prong of the investigation, needed to reconstruct the crib and bedding to determine whether David could have become wedged between the mattress and crib rails.

The detectives interviewed Darlene and Donald, repeating the line of inquiry Hassey had pursued earlier in the day. Darlene again stated that David had been put to bed at 8:30 P.M. and had slept until 5:30. Darlene reported that when Donald had left for work at 6:00 A.M., David had been sleeping and was breathing.

Child abuse investigators are trained to look for inconsistencies. If the nature of the injury does not match the parents' explanation, the investigator assumes that the injury or harm was inflicted or that the parents are lying. Hassey's first interview gave him few clues, but the medical examiner and the police were beginning to put together a picture that yielded some inconsistencies.

Hassey interviewed both parents a second time on October 18, two days after David's death. Darlene still maintained that David was a happy baby with no problems whatsoever, and that he had slept through the night. Hassey wondered whether this was possible, considering the uncomfortable presence of the hard feces in David's bowel.

Meanwhile, the police detectives had uncovered new information. An interview with a neighbor revealed that Darlene had been working as a prostitute out of her apartment and that she had invited a "trick" in after Donald had left for work. The trick was also interviewed and he reported that David was alive and awake at 6:30 A.M.

The medical examiner had determined that David had not suffered any internal hemorrhage, that he had no congenital disorders of his brain, heart, or lungs, and there was no trauma to suggest he had choked on an object. Evidence of his prior elbow fracture, now healed, along with a variety of bruising increased the medical examiner's suspicions. Specifically, of the twelve oval-shaped bruises on David's back, two were seven or more days old, four were four to seven days old, two were one to four days old, and four were so recent they had not begun the color changes that permit dating. Spacing and position of the four sets of bruises (by date) were consistent with a pattern formed by an adult hand without palm pressure. Moreover, the bruises were inconsistent in shape with any toys or other objects found in David's crib.

The detectives' second interview with Darlene resulted in her confession that she had held David down and said "You have to go to sleep, baby." This admission, plus the medical examiner's observations and the hyperinflated lungs, permitted the examiner to rule that David had been suffocated by his mother around 7:00 A.M. on October 16. He became the sixteenth child to be fatally maltreated in the state that year.

Hassey closed the books on the Edwards family by arranging for David's funeral. It was Hassey who went to the funeral home and picked out a small white casket. It was Hassey who made the burial arrangements with the funeral director, and it was Hassey who selected the plot in a local public cemetery where David would be laid to rest. Hassey arranged for the bill of $2,100 to be sent to the Department of Children and Their Families. Three people attended David's burial: his grandparents and Ron Hassey.

Darlene was charged with murder, pleaded guilty to manslaughter, and was sentenced to thirty years—twenty-six of which were to be suspended with supervised probation. As of this writing, she has served her sentence and has been released from prison.

A Preventable Tragedy

This book examines the brief life of David Edwards, one of the three million children reported as being abused or neglected and one of the 1,200 children who are killed by their parents or caretakers in the United States each year. David's case illuminates the grave danger that far too many children experience in this country. It also provides a window on the child welfare system.

David, like nearly half the children killed by their parents or caretakers, had been reported as an abused child and his family had been served by the state child welfare system. Although David's older sister had been abused so severely that Darlene and David Edwards had lost custody of the baby girl, and although David had twice been reported as being abused, he remained with his parents. David's death can be traced to the doctrine that requires social service agencies such as the Department of Children and Their Families to make "reasonable efforts" to keep or reunite abused and neglected children with their biological parents. It can also be traced to the larger ideology behind "reasonable efforts," the sacrosanct belief that children *always* (or nearly always) are better off with their biological parents.

On one level, we might say that nothing could have prevented David Edwards's murder, the act of a depressed and unstable mother. On another level, his death was entirely preventable. As I hope to show, David should not have been allowed to remain in the care of his mother. Numerous warning signs provided opportunities to remove him from harm's way.

At the end of the four months I spent investigating David Edwards's death and interviewing those who were involved with the Edwards family, I became convinced that the system was just as responsible for his death as the actual perpetrator. While we may not be able to change people like Darlene, we could and should have prevented the death of her little boy.

In the years after David's death, I investigated many other child fatalities, reexamined my research on child abuse and neglect, and interviewed and corresponded with countless people in the child welfare system. Again and again I encountered tragedies that could have been prevented if only we did not embrace the rigid policy of family preservation and family reunification.

THE MEDIA SPOTLIGHT

Individual cases of child abuse have captured public attention since the 1800s. One of the best-chronicled cases is that of Mary Ellen Wilson. In 1874 the then eight-year-old Mary Ellen lived in the home of Francis and Mary Connolly, but was not the blood relative of either. Mary Ellen was the illegitimate daughter of Mary Connolly's first husband.[1] A neighbor noticed the plight of Mary Ellen, who was beaten with a leather thong and allowed to go ill-clothed in bad weather. The neighbor reported the case to Etta Wheeler—a "friendly visitor" who worked for St. Luke's Methodist Mission. In the mid-1800s, child welfare was church-based rather than government-based. Etta Wheeler sought help for Mary Ellen from the police and the New York City Department of Charities, but she was turned down—first by the police, who said there was no proof of a crime, and second by the charity agency, who said they did not have custody of Mary Ellen.

Mary Ellen's case received detailed and continuous coverage in the New York daily papers.[2] Legend has it that Henry Berge, founder of the Society for the Prevention of Cruelty to Animals, ultimately intervened on Mary Ellen's behalf and persuaded the courts to accept the case because she was a member of the animal kingdom. What actually happened is that the court chose to review the case because the child needed protection. The case itself was argued, not by Henry Berge and the SPCA, but by Berge's colleague Elbridge Gerry.[3]

Mary Ellen was removed from her foster home and initially placed in an orphanage. Her foster mother was imprisoned for a year. In December 1874, the New York Society for the Prevention of Cruelty to Children was founded in response to the Mary Ellen Wilson case.

Her case is instructive for a number of reasons. First, it illustrates how the story of a single victim can galvanize an otherwise apathetic media and public into active concern about a social problem. The phenomenon of a single case doing more to capture public attention and concern than could be accomplished by mountains of scientific data is not unique to the issue of child abuse. Public awareness of domestic violence increased dramatically after the airing of the fact-based television movie *The Burning Bed* in 1984, and reached an all-time high during saturation media coverage of the murder of Nicole Brown Simpson and Ronald Goldman in June 1994 and the trial of O. J. Simpson. Attention to the issue of missing children intensified as a result of the 1981 abduction and murder of a six-year-old Florida boy, Adam Walsh, and the subsequent airing of the television docudrama about the case. AIDS achieved increased visibility in 1985 when the actor Rock Hudson admitted he had the disease, and again in 1991 when the basketball star Magic Johnson revealed that he was HIV-positive.

Those concerned with airline safety note that progress often comes after a deadly plane crash. Just as the broken and burned bodies of crash victims inspire air safety improvements, so too the shattered bodies and minds of child abuse victims inspire advances in child protection methods.

Publicity alone, however, galvanizes attention for only a short period of time. The duration of sensational stories, such as those of Mary Ellen Wilson, Nicole Brown Simpson, or Magic Johnson, is relatively brief, and soon another social issue or another case takes the spotlight. However, the initial furor can set changes in motion. The case of Mary Ellen Wilson indirectly led to the establishment of the Society for the Prevention of Cruelty to Children. The movie *The Burning Bed* helped pave the way for the use of the "battered women's defense" in state courts. The murder of Nicole Brown Simpson was partially responsible for the passage of numerous state laws pertaining to violence against women and also the final passage of the federal Violence Against Women Act in the summer of 1994.

The case of Mary Ellen Wilson also demonstrates how the facts of a story can be shaped and molded to fit public stereotypes and social advocacy about a social problem. The legend about Mary Ellen being represented by the SPCA because she belonged to the animal kingdom dramatically highlighted the lack of child-focused social protection programs—even though the story was not accurate.

The most significant part of Mary Ellen's story is the part that is least well known: what happened after she was removed from her abusive family. Ironically, the denouement demonstrates both that the child protection system can work *and* that children do not necessarily have to be reunited or remain with their parents in order to develop into caring and productive adults.

Charity worker Etta Wheeler placed Mary Ellen first with Miss Wheeler's mother in Rochester, New York. Mary Ellen was raised by Etta's sister after the death of Mrs. Wheeler. Mary Ellen eventually married Lewis Schutt. Schutt was a widower and had worked as a railroad flagman and gardener; he had two sons from a former marriage. Mary Ellen and Schutt had two daughters, one of whom, Florence Brasser, earned a reputation as one of the best teachers in the city and was honored by having an elementary school named after her.[4]

The lesser-known story of Mary Ellen clearly illustrates the fact that humane and appropriate intervention can create a safe world for children and that family preservation is not a prerequisite for child safety and optimal child development.

RISK AND HARM: FACT AND FICTION

This book is designed to set the record straight about child abuse, child homicide, and the policies and politics of family preservation and family reunification. Before I do that, I also want to point out that some of the public policy record regarding children is skewed in the first place and that record needs to be set straight as well. Some personal tragedies and social issues steal attention and resources that could be better spent on more pressing problems. A first crucial task in protecting children and creating a safe world for them is to distinguish between real and fictive risks.

Satanic abuse, child abductions, and sexual abuse in nursery schools and day care centers have captured public attention in recent years. Individual personal tragedies have indeed resulted from each of these practices. However, as I will show, some of the personal tragedies alleged are merely urban legends. The statistics cited by alarmists are often merely advocacy statistics with no scientific basis.

Satanic Ritual Abuse

This is the most bizarre of the popular notions about children at risk. To cite one alleged example: In May 1987 a four-year-old boy was seen by a pediatrician in Oude Pekela, an industrial village of 8,000 in northeast Holland, for bleeding of the anus.[5] Over the next few days the boy told a story of sexual abuse, including having sticks inserted in his anus. Seventeen police officers were initially involved in the investigation, and ninety-eight children ages four to eleven were interviewed. The children made vague accusations against adults and other children in the community. Some children described watching a videotape and seeing friends on the screen. Others said parties were held where the children were told to undress. They also told of having feces rubbed on them, being urinated on, and being forced to remove feces from the anus of an adult. They said they saw a dead baby in a plastic bag whom they were forced to hit with sticks. The list of bizarre events continued. A number of children spoke of a brown-skinned, deformed child, about six years old, who had a yellow cross placed on his chest. The boy's chest was then cut open and something reddish brown was taken out and placed in a little box.

Clinicians in the United States have also reported cases of ritualistic or satanic abuse, including forced drug usage, sexual abuse, witnessing or receiving physical abuse and torture, witnessing animal mutilations and killings, being buried alive, adult murder, "marriages" to Satan, forced impregnation and sacrifice of one's own child, and forced cannibalism.[6]

A number of clinicians and researchers believe that cases such as these are evidence of a vast international, multigenerational conspiracy practicing religious worship of Satan through sex and death rituals involving torture, incest, perverted sex, animal and human sacrifice, cannibalism, and necrophilia.[7]

Although a small industry of seminars and training sessions on ritual and satanic abuse has developed over the past few years, the actual scholarly documentation and verification of this conspiracy is minimal. Not a single case of satanic murder, human sacrifice, or cannibalism has been documented. The psychiatrist Frank Putnam, of the National Institute of Mental Health, asserts flat out that the cases presented are not readily believable.[8] The sociologist David Bromly argues it is inconceivable that a vast underground network of satanic cultists operating since the 1950s would fail to produce a single defector who has hard evidence of their existence.[9]

What is the truth? Is ritualistic or satanic abuse a significant harm that befalls children? Is the chaos that follows investigations of allegations of satanic abuse a justifiable consequence of a needed effort to protect children? Roland Summit, a respected researcher in the field of sexual abuse, believes that as many as a hundred children each year are subjected to bizarre ritualistic abuse, and that is a tragedy for the children and their families. But a hundred children is not a social problem that warrants enormous commitments of social resources to prevent or treat.

Abducted Children

Six-year-old Etan Patz had pleaded with his mother that he was old enough to walk to the bus stop alone. On the morning of May 25, 1979, he left his Prince Street apartment in the SoHo section of New York City for school. His mother watched him cross the street from the window of her apartment. Etan walked out of his mother's view on his way to the bus stop and was never seen again. It was one of the most publicized missing-child cases in the country. The New York newspapers covered it closely, and Etan's picture appeared in the papers, on post office bulletin boards, and on milk cartons for years, but no trace of him was ever discovered.

The Patz case, along with that of Adam Walsh two years later, stimulated widespread, intense anxiety about the risk of child abduction. John Walsh, Adam's father, became an outspoken crusader on behalf of parents whose children had disappeared or been kidnapped. Congress held hearings on the problem of missing children from 1981 to 1985. Academics joined the crusade. The sociologist Michael Agopian testified that tens of thousands of Adams existed whose cases were not prominently reported by the media.[10] John Walsh testified that the country was littered with mutilated, decapitated, raped, and strangled children. Etan's mother, Julie Patz, was appointed to the U.S. Attorney General's Advisory Committee Board on Missing Children.

Perhaps the most significant event in establishing the threat of child kidnapping was the broadcast of *Adam,* the TV movie about the Walsh case, on October 10, 1983. The program elicited thousands of phone calls, some of which, it was claimed, led to the discovery of missing children. In the wake of the broadcast, the private National Center for Missing and Exploited Children was opened in 1984 and continues to be funded by the U.S. Department of Justice.

In a comparatively short period of time, the threat of abduction was catapulted to prominence as a serious one. If the cases of Etan Patz, Adam Walsh, and other missing children were not enough to attract the public's and policymakers' attention, the often told story of an anonymous child kidnapped from a shopping mall (or in some versions, Disneyworld or Disneyland) did the trick. In the story, a little girl, perhaps three or four years old, is left unattended for a moment in the mall. When the parent looks for the girl, she is missing. The parent yells, "Help, my child is missing," and the mall security guards quickly lock the exits and begin their search. After a while, they find the child. Her hair has been cut and she has been changed from her dress into a shirt and slacks. The kidnappers clearly had intended to disguise the girl as a boy and make their escape. In another version of the story, the kidnappers cut the child's hair and change her clothes while she is on a ride in an amusement park. These stories are meant to underscore the danger that lurks in public places and the need to take the threat of kidnapping seriously. The sociologist Joel Best refers to such stories as "urban legends."[11] These legends are used by what Best "claims-makers" to mobilize concern and support to fight the alleged social problem.

A second form of claims-making is the use of statistics on the extent of the problem. Those testifying before congressional committees on the issue of child abductions and missing children claimed that thousands of children were missing. One common estimate was that 25,000 to 50,000 youngsters were kidnapped by strangers each year. Some claims-makers even went so far as to state that there were 1.8 million missing children—but this estimate included runaways and abductions by parents.

Despite these claims, Federal Bureau of Investigation records document a maximum of seventy child kidnap victims investigated in a year and an average of about fifty child kidnappings a year.[12] The FBI estimated that between 43 and 147 children were abducted and murdered by strangers between 1976 and 1987, for an average of 4 to 15 each year.

The numbers of missing children simply do not add up to a major social harm that requires a significant investment of public and private resources. The pictures on the milk cartons, the efforts of socially active businesses and civic groups to fingerprint young children, and the other campaigns aimed at reducing child kidnapping are out of proportion to the risk to the nation's children. Again, I am not minimizing the grief suffered by those families whose children have been abducted, nor do I advocate that nothing be done, but I believe that the time, attention, and resources devoted to this problem should be proportional to the true extent of the problem, not to the public hysteria.

Sexual Abuse in Day Care Centers

Although children have probably been sexually abused in day care centers for years, it was the McMartin Preschool case in Manhattan Beach, California, that did the most to draw attention to issues and anxieties surrounding this problem.[13] In August 1983, a parent of a child at the McMartin Preschool told police that her son had been sexually abused by Raymond Buckey, a teacher at the school and grandson of its founder. Buckey was first arrested and then released for lack of evidence. The police then sent letters to more than 200 parents stating that Raymond Buckey might have molested their children. The police were swamped with calls by parents who either feared that their children had been abused or who claimed they had indeed been. The owner of the school, Peggy McMartin Buckey, along with Ray Buckey and six others were indicted and charged with 300 counts involving 100 children. Press coverage of the case was exhaustive, including accounts on the national TV news, *Nightline,* and national news magazines; an HBO docudrama about the case, *Indictment,* was broadcast in May 1995.

Parents want to believe that day care centers and nursery schools are nurturing environments staffed by caring people. Questions about the safety of day care centers and nursery schools violate parents' hopes of a secure world for their children and themselves.

The alleged perpetrators in the McMartin case were found innocent after lengthy and costly trials. The various trials went on for six years and at an estimated cost of $16 million—the costliest trials in U.S. history at the time. Some observers pilloried the clinicians involved in the case as being overzealous in their attempt to elicit stories of victimization from the children.[14] The public, of course, was left almost in the dark. Were their fears about the risk of sexual abuse in day care facilities justified? Were day care centers and nursery schools staffed by pedophiles who were attracted by a setting that offered them easy access to child victims, or was the issue the creation of fanatical clinicians and a gullible media and public?

Day care crimes are not the plague the media painted them to be in the early 1980s, nor are they merely isolated incidents experienced by a just a few children. The sociologist David Finkelhor and his associates concluded that sexual abuse is not as likely in day care centers as it is in families, but its occurrence in centers is not trivial either.[15] Nearly 31 out of 10,000 day care centers in the United States have had documented cases of child sexual abuse. A little more than 5 children per 10,000 (six years old or younger) enrolled in day care centers are reported as sexually abused each year. The researchers conclude that although a day care center is more likely to be reported for child sexual abuse than a family is, a given child has a lower risk of being abused in a day care center than in his or her own home.

These crimes are more than personal tragedies. The young age of the victims, the difficulties of conducting investigations, and the sometimes unusual and even bizarre nature of the abuse as well as multiple victimization by one offender are causes for deep concern. However, the high emotions that surround day care sexual abuse should not be allowed to generate alarmist or poorly considered policies that might be damaging in the long run.[16]

FOCUSING ENERGY AND RESOURCES

Claims-making on behalf of children has become a double-edged sword. The often sensational and always emotional cases of harm done to children like Mary Ellen Wilson, Lisa Steinberg in New York in 1987, and Susan Smith's two sons in Union, South Carolina, in 1994 capture the attention, hearts, and often the purse strings of professionals, policymakers, and the public. The case of Mary Ellen Wilson did lead to the founding of the Society for the Prevention of Cruelty to Children, and to increased awareness of child abuse.

But the use of dubious numbers and urban legends to arouse an apathetic citizenry and seemingly indifferent legislative bodies eventually becomes the equivalent of the boy who cried wolf, so that real harm and risk to children are not recognized or attended to. False claims-making means that the limited resources available to protect children from harm will be spread too thin and the children who are truly in need of help will be overlooked.

The abuse and murder of children are major social problems, public health threats to children, and crimes that require strong and effective response. The child welfare system, which was instituted to protect children, continues to fail them. The problem is not simply that resources are lacking, but that the central mission of child welfare agencies, preserving families, does not work and places many children at significant risk of continued injury and death.

I offer no simple solutions to the problem of child abuse but a detailed look at how the child welfare system handled one family and how the structure, function, and mission of the system kept one child in harm's way instead of protecting him.

Although the story of David Edwards is one of despair, my hope is that a careful examination of David's case, the child welfare system, and national child protection policies can lead to a safer world for children.

2

Sentinels:
Monitoring Child Safety

LOOKING BACK ON THE RECORD, ONE CAN SEE THAT THE tragedy of David Edwards actually began before he was born. The first contact the Edwards family had with the child welfare system occurred when David's older sister, Marie, was only six weeks old.

Some aspects of the child welfare system do work some of the time to protect children, as the early stages of the Edwards case show. Perhaps the most efficient and effective component of the system is the network of "sentinels" who are legally responsible for identifying cases of suspected child abuse and neglect and reporting them to state agencies for investigation, assessment, and, if needed, services.[1] The network of community sentinels is generally composed of those professionals who have regular and close contact with children and who are trained to identify signs of suspected maltreatment. Physicians and other medical professionals are the backbone of the sentinel system, but teachers, counselors, school nurses, principals, day care providers, social workers, and police officers are also counted on to man the watchtowers.

Of the entire system the Edwards family was involved with over two and a half years, the sentinel system worked the best, and even it had a significant crack that Marie Edwards nearly fell through. In David's case, the crack became a gap the size of the Grand Canyon.

A YOUNG FAMILY

Marie Edwards was born April 10, 1988, the first child of Darlene and Donald Edwards. Darlene, twenty-one years old, grew up in a blue-collar suburb, one of six children in a large Catholic extended family. Her father abandoned the family when Darlene was five; her mother remarried shortly thereafter.

Darlene's stepfather was an alcoholic who delighted in verbally abusing the children—"busting their balls," as Darlene described it. He was also extremely restrictive, often confining the children to their bedrooms for hours as punishment for even minor misbehavior. He used physical punishment as well, although the level of violence was never enough to cause a significant injury or lead to a report for child abuse. Of course, this was before the mandatory child abuse reporting laws. According to one study of reporting, the state where Darlene Edwards grew up had not a single confirmed report of child abuse in either 1967 or 1968![2]

Her mother described Darlene as a wild teenager who liked to party, drink, and smoke pot. She did poorly in high school, finally dropping out. None of Darlene's drinking, pot smoking, or partying ever brought her into contact with the police, and her various transgressions in school were minor ones resulting either in detention or short-term suspensions. Darlene may have been a "wild teenager," but not one who was ever classified as delinquent or violent.

Donald Edwards, twenty-six years old when Marie was born, also was one of six children, also described his father as an alcoholic, and, like Darlene's father, Donald's father abandoned his family, when Donald was eleven. Donald's mother, who was also an alcoholic, remarried four years after her husband's departure. Donald's stepfather had little influence on Donald, as he was a truck driver and away from home much of the time.

Donald completed high school, but afterward got into trouble from time to time. Donald described ten arrests for various crimes over a six-year period, including several for possession of marijuana and other controlled substances. Donald claimed that he did not have an alcohol or drug problem, although he drank on occasion and, from accounts that emerged during the investigation of the circumstances of David's death, used marijuana and possibly also sold marijuana from time to time.

Darlene and Donald were married in August 1986 and rented an apartment in the city. Darlene held various jobs, including sales clerk and waitress, while Donald worked for a jewelry manufacturer. Although the Edwardses were hardly wealthy, they lived well above the poverty line.

At some point during their marriage, probably before Marie was born, Darlene, with Donald's apparent knowledge and approval, began to supplement her income by working as a prostitute out of their apartment. It is not unusual to find that mothers whose children are severely abused or killed worked for a time as prostitutes. What was unusual about the Edwards family was that the parents were married, the husband held a steady job, the income was above the poverty level, and the drug use was confined to marijuana.

Darlene became pregnant about eleven months after she was married. Marie was born apparently healthy and was taken to a pediatrician for the normal "well baby" visits. Darlene, however, suffered extreme postpartum depression. She had stopped working when Marie was born and her main sources of contact and support were her mother and stepfather, who lived about a half hour away. Darlene's contacts with her family were largely confined to phone calls. Since Donald did not get along with Darlene's mother and stepfather, Darlene's family rarely visited. Darlene sometimes took Marie to her mother's home, and her mother and stepfather baby-sat Marie from time to time.

Although some parents can be identified as possibly abusive as early as the pregnancy or delivery, many others who become abusers cannot be accurately identified by the sentinels at the time the baby is born.[3] At the time Marie was born, a sentinel observing the family would not necessarily have predicted that she was at risk. As noted, some of the prime risk factors for severe abuse (single mother, poverty, drug abuse) were not present. Although Donald and Darlene had experienced physical punishment and emotional abuse themselves, neither had been officially identified as abused children. On the other hand, some risk factors *were* present. Darlene's depression and isolation were the most notable early warning signs.

THE PHYSICIAN'S DUTY TO REPORT

Marie's Doctor

Early on the morning of May 23, Darlene called her pediatrician, Jo Systram, and asked for an immediate appointment. She wasn't specific about what was so urgent, but implied that her baby, Marie, had not eaten for two days.

Dr. Systram concluded that Marie's eating problem was the result of severe head trauma. She had a subdural hematoma, a swelling of the brain, as well as fractures of her legs and ribs. When the doctor asked Darlene how Marie had been injured, she made a vague reference to a fall. Dr. Systram told Darlene that the injury was severe and to take Marie to the hospital immediately.

Nearly three hours passed between the time Darlene, who had arrived in her own car, left Dr. Systram's office with Marie and the time she showed up at the emergency room, a mile or so away. It is not clear what happened during those hours. One thing is clear: Six-week-old Marie, badly injured, was in so much pain that she probably could not have been comforted by her mother. The hours Darlene spent with Marie must have been extremely stressful for both of them.

The emergency room team confirmed the diagnosis of fractured ribs, legs, and the subdural hematoma. A complete examination also revealed a number of bruises on the baby's tiny body. They were in various stages of healing, thus indicating injuries that had occurred on several occasions over the past days and weeks.

The state child abuse law allowed the hospital to hold Marie for the next seventy-two hours. She was admitted and a day later, a physician at the hospital reported the case to the Child Abuse and Neglect Tracking System (CANTS) unit of the Department of Children and Their Families (DCF).

Dr. Systram should have immediately filed a Physician's Report of Examination as required by state law and reported Marie Edwards as a suspected abuse victim to the CANTS unit herself. Child abuse laws in all fifty states require physicians to report suspected abuse. Dr. Systram should also have arranged for transport to the hospital for Darlene and Marie. Even though Darlene might not have fit the profile of the typical abuser, the severity of Marie's head injury and the lack of an adequate explanation for it were significant enough to warrant quick action by Dr. Systram. Dr. Systram was a well-trained, competent professional. She was young enough to have received her medical training after mandatory child abuse reporting statutes had been enacted. Although medical schools do not include a great deal about child abuse in their curriculum, the smattering of training opportunities they do provide and the discussion of child abuse in the profession would give most pediatricians at least a passing knowledge of the phenomenon and their obligation to report suspected abuse or neglect. Moreover, since a handful of malpractice suits have been won against physicians who failed to report suspected cases of child abuse, it is reasonable to assume that most pediatricians would take care to report suspected cases so as to reduce any liability they might have should further harm befall their patients. Finally, the state also had a criminal liability provision in the reporting law for anyone who failed to report a suspected case of child abuse. The unwillingness of private physicians and other mandated reporters to report abuse and neglect is one of the most serious fissures in the child welfare system.

Albert Huey, the child protection investigator assigned to the case, made an appointment to see Dr. Systram five days after Marie was admitted to the hospital. As soon as Huey entered Dr. Systram's office, she said: "I thought I'd be hearing from DCF—that baby was a battered child."

The most unusual aspect of Huey's interview with Dr. Systram was that he realized no information would have been forthcoming from her had he not called for an appointment to interview her about Marie. Huey was nonplused by the enormous contradiction between Dr. Systram's claim that Marie was one of the worst cases of child battering she had ever seen and her failure to file a child abuse report with DCF. Perhaps the doctor assumed that Darlene would take Marie to the emergency room immediately and that the physicians there would, upon recognizing the seriousness of the injuries, take the responsibility for filing the report. Dr. Systram must also have assumed that Darlene would indeed be concerned enough to take Marie to the emergency room in the first place. Whatever the reason—and Huey never did ask—no report was filed by Dr. Systram.

Dr. Systram's failure to file a report was a crack in the system, a crack that could have had fatal consequences for Marie. However, since no harm resulted from the doctor's failure to report Marie as an abused child, no one took action to punish Dr. Systram for nonfeasance.

David's Doctor

The Edwards family's second assessment by a physician began shortly after the birth of David. It was this assessment that could have, and should have, saved his life. David Edwards was born July 5, 1989, fifteen months after his sister Marie was born. Darlene's pregnancy and delivery were unremarkable and David was, by all accounts, also a normal baby, weighing eight pounds, eight ounces. Darlene and Donald chose another pediatrician for David, preferring, not surprisingly, to avoid Dr. Systram. Darlene took David for his first visit to Dr. Alice Tanner when he was three weeks old. Dr. Tanner was unaware that David had an older sister who had been seriously abused and injured at six weeks of age and was in foster care.

David weighed nine and a half pounds at that first visit: he had gained nearly a full pound in the three weeks since he was born. The checkup was a routine well-baby visit; Dr. Tanner's notes indicated that David "looked OK, was gaining weight and doing well, but was a bit irritable."

At his next monthly well-baby visit he appeared healthy and was gaining weight. Dr. Tanner saw no signs of risk and had no concerns or suspicions about David's health and well-being.

David's third visit to his pediatrician, at three months of age, generated the first small signs of concern. First, when Dr. Tanner's nurse weighed him, he was under twelve pounds, a loss of a pound. This amount of weight loss in a one-month period is unusual, especially since there had been no calls or visits about illness or gastrointestinal disturbance. A weight loss of a pound in a baby who should have *gained* a pound or more in a month would be considered a sign of "nonorganic failure to thrive," a form of child neglect. Such a diagnosis requires other information. Dr. Tanner thought that perhaps the weight recorded at the visit a month earlier might have been in error, and that David had not really lost weight.

During this visit Darlene discussed how anxious she was about her baby. She said she was "very concerned" about him and often stayed up at night watching him breathe to make sure he was OK. Darlene also said she was beginning to feel "kind of trapped" at home all day with her baby. Her apparent depression was a second risk factor for possible abuse and neglect.

Dr. Tanner was concerned about the two risk markers, but

she did not have enough information to warrent intervention, so she took the prudent course of scheduling Darlene and David to return in two weeks. This way, at least, she could monitor David's weight and Darlene's depression.

After these first small signs, no additional physical or developmental warnings occurred over the next six months. David was developing normally, both physically and socially. One small concern to Dr. Tanner was that Darlene would occasionally say she was not getting enough time away from David. David's weight did fluctuate, increasing Dr. Tanner's worry about failure to thrive. But just as she would begin to consider filing a report, David would gain weight and this would quell her suspicions about possible neglect.

Dr. Tanner did observe a small bruise on David during his eight-month visit. The bruise was small, about a half centimeter, on his right upper arm. There were no other bruises on his body.

During this visit, Dr. Tanner referred Darlene to a social worker at the hospital with which Dr. Tanner was affiliated—the same hospital that had treated Marie—to discuss Darlene's irritability and feelings of being cooped up with David. Darlene met with the social worker a couple of times.

The next month, Dr. Tanner noticed some new marks: a small bruise over David's right temple, and some small, broken blood vessels, or petechiae, on his left forearm. Darlene said she hadn't noticed either and provided no explanation for where the bruises came from.

Dr. Tanner scheduled the next visit for two weeks hence, a

bit worried about the small bruises and broken blood vessels, even though nothing about these injuries suggested they were other than the normal bumps and bruises kids get.

Anonymous Calls

When David was nine months old, the CANTS hotline received an anonymous call reporting that a David Edwards was "pale and skinny" and had incurred a "chipped elbow" the previous November. The caller claimed that David Edwards's parents were "violent" and that an older child had been removed from the parents because of physical abuse. Six weeks later, on June 5, another anonymous caller (probably the same person) said that David was "failing."

MANDATORY-REPORTING LAWS

Between 1963 and 1967 every state and the District of Columbia passed some form of child abuse reporting law. According to the public policy expert Barbara Nelson, these reporting laws diffused through the states five times faster than the average for public policy innovations between 1933 and 1966. There are various explanations for this speed. Certainly a model reporting law disseminated by the United States Children's Bureau, an agency within the then Department of Health, Education and Welfare, facilitated the states' rapid adoption of reporting laws. Other model laws were drafted by the Council of State Governments, the American Medical

Association, and the American Academy of Pediatrics. Rather than confusing the state governments, these various model laws seemed to, in Nelson's words, "superheat" the demands for legislation.[4]

Mandatory-reporting laws had a number of attractive features. First, they "legalized" the problem of child abuse. Second, mandatory-reporting laws were a sign that state government was "doing something" about the problem. Third, and not a trivial factor, was that of all the policy options available, reporting laws appeared to be the least expensive that could address the problem. The last assumption proved to be inaccurate. Physicians, legislators, and government officials had dramatically underestimated the extent of the problem of child abuse and the demand for services that would result from the reporting laws.

Estimates of the Extent of Child Abuse and Neglect: 1960s–1970s

Those pushing for reporting laws believed such laws would help identify abused and neglected children who needed protection and abusive families that needed help. Everyone involved in the early efforts to enact reporting laws assumed that the problem of abuse and neglect was large enough to warrant the laws but small enough to be managed by existing human service and medical systems. A nationwide inventory in 1967 of reported cases of child abuse found 6,000 confirmed cases. But a second part of the study, which asked a representative sample of 1,520 adults whether they had personal knowledge of families where incidents of child abuse had occurred, found that forty-five respondents, or 3 percent of the sample, reported knowledge of forty-eight different incidents: extrapolating this number to a national population of 110 million adults, the researcher estimated that between 2.53 million and 4.07 million children were abused each year.[5] Another survey of community agencies that have contact with abused children, in the early 1970s, estimated there were 950,000 reportable cases of abuse and neglect each year, two-thirds of which were reported and one-third of which were not.[6] A physician placed the figure as high as 1.5 million in 1973.[7] These estimates of millions of cases were viewed by most as exaggerated. In testimony before the United States Senate in 1973, for example, an American Humane Association official estimated that there were 30,000 to 40,000 truly abused children in the United States.[8]

The early experiences with mandatory reporting seemed to confirm the conservative estimates about the extent of child abuse. Of course, in the first few years after the laws were enacted, little effort was expended to educate professionals and the public about their reporting obligations. Only a small number of professionals actually knew about the laws, fewer knew to whom they had to make a report, and even fewer reported.

But in the early 1970s, campaigns were launched to improve professional and public awareness of child abuse and the reporting laws. At the same time, technology in the form of WATS lines and 800 numbers allowed professionals and concerned citizens to make toll-free long distance calls to file reports.

The combined results of the public awareness campaigns and improved telecommunications technology had a stunning effect. In Florida, the number of reports increased from 17 to 19,000 in one year (1970) after a state-wide toll-free telephone number for reporting suspected cases was installed and a mass media campaign alerted people to the existence of the toll-free number.[9]

Not until 1976 was an effort made to tabulate national statistics on child abuse and neglect reporting. The newly formed National Center on Child Abuse and Neglect (then in the Department of Health, Education and Welfare; now in the Department of Health and Human Services) provided a grant to the American Humane Association to collect reporting data from each state. In 1976, the first year data were collected, 669,000 reports of child abuse and neglect were recorded nationwide. This was a far larger number than had been expected but still quite a bit smaller than the estimates of millions being made by some researchers around this same time. Child abuse reports did exceed 1 million by 1980, were greater than 1.5 million in 1984, and topped 2 million in 1986. In 1993, there were 2,936,554 children reported as abused or neglected.[10]

From the time they were first tabulated, there has been a 327 percent increase in reports of child abuse and neglect. The bad news was that the extent of the problem exceeded even the highest estimates of the early 1970s. The good news was that the reporting laws seemed to be working. Each year more and more children in harm's way were coming to public attention.

The good news, however, was not as good as it seemed.

Even the more than 2 million reports did not represent all the cases of abused and neglected children. Dr. Systram's inaction was less the exception and closer to the rule.

IS CHILD ABUSE AND NEGLECT UNDERREPORTED?

In 1980, the first National Study of the Incidence and Severity of Child Abuse and Neglect estimated that only one out of three cases of child abuse was reported to child welfare agencies.[11]

A survey conducted in the mid-1980s by the psychologist Gail Zellman of nearly 1,200 mandated reporters, including general and family practitioners, pediatricians, child psychiatrists, clinical psychologists, social workers, school principals, and heads of child care centers, found that more than three-quarters had made child abuse reports at some time in their professional careers. Although the reporting rate varied by profession, with elementary school principals having the highest likelihood of ever reporting a suspected case and child care providers having the lowest likelihood, there is clear evidence that most mandated professionals understand their reporting obligations and act on them. For most of the professionals surveyed, reporting was neither a distant nor a rare event. More than half had reported a case of abuse in the year prior to the survey.[12]

However, having ever reported a suspected case of abuse is not the same as reporting *all* cases. Forty percent of the mandated reporters surveyed said that they had, at some time in their professional careers, failed to report a suspected case of child abuse. In other words, given that reporting laws require reports of all suspected cases of abuse, the professionals admitted to violating laws. More than one in five of the mandated reporters (22 percent) said they failed to report a case of suspected abuse just in the year prior to the survey.

There are a number of reasons a mandated reporter would fail to report a suspected case of abuse. The reason cited most often in Zellman's survey was the professional's belief that the evidence was not sufficient to warrant a report. More often than not, this meant that the professional believed the injury or condition was not serious enough to be reported. But the reporting laws require professionals to report *suspected* cases, not proven cases, of maltreatment. The burden of investigation, assessment, and validation is on the child welfare agencies, not on the reporter.

A second influential rationale for nonreporting is the belief that the professional can do more to help the child and family than the child protection agency could. A number of the nonreporting professionals in Zellman's survey stated that child protection workers overreact to reports and/or their services are of poor quality. The case of Marie and David Edwards offers clear evidence to support the second belief: agency assessments and services can be of poor quality and can, in fact, be more harmful to a child and family than helpful.

A smaller proportion of professionals offered a third set of explanations for their failure to report suspected cases of abuse or neglect: that reporting would be bad for them. These professionals stated that filing reports and being interviewed for assessments took too much time. Moreover, there was always the chance that the reporting professional would have to appear in one or more court proceedings regarding the case. These professionals also feared lawsuits for false reports, although all state reporting statutes protect mandated reporters from lawsuits if their report is made in good faith. Some mandated reporters confessed that they would feel uncomfortable in their dealings with a family afterward if they filed an abuse report. Finally, a small number of reporters in Zellman's survey confessed that they were not sure how to make a report or would not make one because it would breach confidentiality.

Dr. Systram's reasons for not reporting Marie's injuries were most likely related to this "it's bad for me" set of explanations for not reporting.

Nearly thirty years after the implementation of child abuse and neglect reporting laws, not all vulnerable children are coming to the attention of the agencies responsible for investigating suspected cases of abuse and providing services. The sentinels are still not entirely fulfilling their obligations on behalf of children in harm's way.

Is Child Abuse and Neglect Overreported?

Answering the question about underreporting does not automatically provide an answer about overreporting. The emergency room report on Marie Edwards was one of nearly 3 million such reports received by child welfare agencies in the United States each year. The lesser-known statistic is that not all 3 million reports are, after investigation, considered substantiated, founded, or valid reports.

Not every report of suspected abuse and neglect is even investigated. Some calls, because of the demeanor of the caller or the nature of the information provided, are screened out before investigation. The availability of 800 numbers and the public awareness campaigns conducted nationally and in many states produce a number of "crank" reports. Some calls describe instances that are not legally abuse and neglect, while others involve alleged perpetrators who are not covered by abuse and neglect laws (perpetrators must be caretakers or individuals in caretaking positions). Apart from the marginal, crank, or otherwise inappropriate calls, the majority of reports *are* assigned for investigation.

Of the 2,936,554 reports of suspected abuse and neglect in 1993, 38 percent were either substantiated or indicated as cases of abuse.[13] This means that the child protection agencies' investigations yielded some credible evidence that the child reported was in fact at risk. The criteria for substantiation vary from state to state. In general, however, a substantiated report means that some level of intervention on behalf of the child is warranted. The designation "substantiated" does not always mean that the child protection agency opens the case for services or provides services. In some instances, services are already being provided by a social service, medical, or other agency.

The best available data suggest that the majority of reports of child abuse and neglect are unsubstantiated. What exactly does this mean? One interpretation of these data is that the 60 percent or so of the reports that are not substantiated after investigation are "false reports." Douglas Besharov, a lawyer and resident scholar at the American Enterprise Institute for Public Policy Research and one of the leading critics of the child welfare system, directs much of his attention to the large number of unsubstantiated, or what he calls "unfounded," reports of abuse and neglect.[14] One of Besharov's main concerns is that the verdict of "unfounded" can be reached only after an unavoidably traumatic investigation that is, in Besharov's view, inherently a breach of parental and family privacy. Not only are family members questioned, but so are friends, relatives, neighbors, schoolteachers, day care providers, doctors, clergy, and many others. The journalist Richard Wexler offers a similar but more graphic critique of those he sarcastically calls "child savers," discussing at length the traumatic investigations of unfounded cases and the harm that befalls children who are inappropriately removed from homes after an unfounded allegation of abuse or neglect.[15]

Besharov, and to a lesser extent, Wexler, make important points. If child abuse and neglect investigations are traumatic, and many are, and if they violate family privacy, which they might, then the annual total of 1.7 million unfounded reported cases of abuse and neglect seems much too high a price to pay for child protection.

The flaw in both Besharov and Wexler's logic is that they seem to equate *unsubstantiated* or *unfounded* with *invalid* and *false*. Just because a report of abuse cannot be determined valid does not mean it is a false report. The dividing line between a substantiated and unsubstantiated case is hardly as clear or definite as those who claim abuse is overreported imply.[16]

One of the unanticipated outcomes of the remarkable increase in media as well as professional attention to child abuse is the belief, held by much of the public and many professionals, that child abuse is nearly always clear-cut. The media tend to focus on the most gruesome and grotesque cases, and frequently illustrate print and television stories about abuse with graphic photographs. The unintended consequence of the gruesome and graphic media presentations is that audiences begin to assume that detecting child abuse is a simple matter of observing handprints on children's faces or backs, cigarette burns on their legs or arms. But the vast majority of abuse cases are not nearly so severe or obvious as the examples displayed in the media. More often than not, a child's injury could just as easily be attributable to an accident. Children do fall down; children do place their hands on hot stoves. Often, the injury itself provides little in the way of insight into cause. As in the case of Marie Edwards, clinicians often base a diagnosis on the nature of the injury and the parents' explanation for how it occurred. Additional information, such as family living circumstances and background, also fill out the picture.

In describing the process of examining children for suspected abuse and neglect, the pediatrician Eli Newberger, one of the nation's leading experts in the field, summarized the problems clinicians face by stating, "We must make hard decisions based on soft data." "Soft" data don't allow child protective investigators to substantiate or validate a report of abuse. Thus a significant portion of the large number of unsubstantiated reports of abuse are not false or invalid reports, but reports for which the clinical, medical, and social data were insufficient to determine clearly whether the child was intentionally injured and is at risk for future harm, as in the case of David Edwards's initial involvement with child welfare sentinels.

Besharov's, and especially Wexler's, inferences about the prevalence of false reports are simply not correct. Given that most abuse takes place in the private and intimate confines of the home, it will always be difficult to prove cases of abuse and neglect conclusively. Furthermore, given the high standards of evidence required by courts, child protective agencies will generally not go forward with a case unless they have adequate evidence to warrant state intervention into the parent–child relationship. Thus high rates of "unsubstantiated" cases are a necessary price for protecting children.

Besharov's claims that child abuse is overreported led to quick and critical response from both the child welfare and research communities. Most of the criticisms focused on the apparent claim that unsubstantiated meant invalid or false reports. The critics, however, generally overlooked a second facet of Besharov's concern about overreporting: The remarkable increase in reporting was clogging the child welfare system with so many cases that it could not adequately serve those children who are at significant risk of harm.[17]

Another, less widely discussed factor in the reporting increase is the broadening of the definition of what constitutes child abuse.

Among the first to systematically study and write about child abuse were the physician C. Henry Kempe and his colleagues. Their seminal 1962 article, "The Battered-Child Syndrome," published in the *Journal of the American Medical Association*, defined abuse as deliberate acts of physical violence that produce diagnosable injuries.[18] Not long after this article appeared, social service personnel began to argue quite strongly that physical injury was not the only harm children suffered that required professional intervention. Children are starved, sent outdoors into freezing weather with inadequate clothing, deprived of medical attention and the opportunity for an education, medicated and sedated needlessly, subjected to cruel mental and emotional abuse, and sexually victimized by adult caretakers. In 1974 the National Center on Child Abuse and Neglect defined child abuse broadly as "the physical or mental injury, sexual abuse, negligent treatment, or maltreatment of a child under the age of eighteen by a person who is responsible for the child's welfare under circumstances which indicate that the child's health or welfare is harmed or threatened thereby (Public Law 93-237)."

This expansion of the definition of child abuse was partially motivated by a sincere desire to expand services for children at risk. The motivation also was the result of tight budgets for social services and the need of social service agencies to demonstrate an expanding caseload as justification for continued or increased funds. Private and public agency administrators knew that few politicians would restrict funding if they were presented with graphic photos of child abuse victims combined with hard data on growing caseloads. Few government officials ever asked about what portion of the caseloads were made up of the children portrayed in the photos—they simply assumed that all the cases reported were similar to the pictures they saw.

The fraying of the social safety net in the 1980s contributed to increased caseloads for child protection agencies. Although the agencies were probably not seeing more cases of severe physical abuse or even fatal child abuse, their caseloads were growing because more and more cases of neglect were taken on by the child protection system.

Of 1,018,692 substantiated or indicated abuse and neglect victims the National Center on Child Abuse and Neglect had records for in 1993 (from forty-nine states submitting reports), 45 percent of reports were for neglect, 22 percent for physical abuse, 13 percent for sexual abuse, and the remaining 20 percent for medical neglect, emotional maltreatment, or other types of maltreatment.[19] No doubt some of the reports of "neglect" were the result of acts of omission that parents could control. However, a substantial portion of those reports simply represented indigent parents and their children being swept up into the child welfare system. Families and children who might have been served by other social agencies and other welfare programs in the 1960s and 1970s were now receiving services by the most readily available means. Of course, the services came with the price tag of an invasive investigation and the stigma of being labeled an abuser.

Thus Besharov is partially correct. Child protection agencies are indeed overburdened by reports and subsequent investigations. And it is likely that those children who are at high risk of further injury are not being properly served by child welfare workers burdened with more and more responsibility for children and families who might be better served by general family support and welfare programs.

CREATING A SAFE WORLD

Thus child abuse and neglect are both overreported and underreported. The solution seems obvious: Increase reporting of valid cases, and reduce the number of inappropriate or invalid reports. This is in fact what Besharov, Wexler, and others suggest. Their solution would be to reduce what social scientists call "false positives," or invalid reports, while at the same time reducing "false negatives"—the incorrect labeling as not at risk of a child who actually is. Social scientists know that this is impossible. One can reduce false positives only at the expense of increasing the likelihood of false negatives. Reducing the vigilance and aggressiveness of mandated reporters would indeed reduce invalid reports, but only at the cost of increasing the number of children who fall through the cracks and escape detection as being at risk.

A safe world for children can only be achieved if child protection agencies and mandated reporters have as their singular goal to reduce false negatives. Child abuse and neglect *are underreported.* Dr. Systram created significant risk for Marie Edwards by failing to fulfill her legal obligation to report suspected child abuse and neglect. The failings of child protection systems notwithstanding, children can be protected only if their vulnerability or injuries come to official attention.

Reporting, however, is not the magic key. If the system were not so clogged, high-risk cases such as Marie and David Edwards might receive effective preventive intervention. The solution, however, is not less reporting. The solution is a better and more accurate means of risk assessment for reported cases.

3

Investigation and Risk Assessment

WITH SENTINELS IN PLACE TO IDENTIFY AND REPORT ABUSE and neglect, the linchpin of child protection is a reliable system of investigation and risk assessment.

Those who report as well as those who investigate abuse all engage in risk assessment. Some agencies and investigators use formal, written procedures. Others rely on clinical judgment, clinical intuition, or just accumulated experience. Training in risk assessment is equally variable. Some child welfare agencies invest considerable resources in training their workers in the area of risk assessment. Other agencies provide only minimal training for new employees and even less ongoing staff training.

The Edwards family was assessed for risk twice. The first assessment began in May 1988 after Marie Edwards was reported to the Child Abuse and Neglect Tracking System (CANTS) unit.

The Investigation of
Marie's Case

Two days after the emergency room doctor reported Marie's case to the CANTS unit, it was assigned to Albert Huey for investigation. Given the severity of Marie's injuries, it might seem remiss of the department to wait two days before assigning the case for investigation. Time, however, was not of the essence here. The case was not classified as an emergency, because no immediate threat or danger to the child was present: Marie was admitted to and being cared for by the hospital. Her injuries would keep her from being sent home quickly.

Because the seventy-two-hour hold the hospital had on Marie would expire May 26, the day the case was assigned to Huey, the department's attorney went before a judge in Family Court and requested an ex parte order that the legal and physical custody of Marie be temporarily transferred to the Department of Children and Their Families (DCF). The attorney presented Dr. Delaney's Physician's Report of Examination as evidence, and custody was immediately granted to the department. An arraignment date for the parents was set for four days later.

Albert Huey, a seasoned and confident professional, had carried out many investigations in his seven years with the CANTS unit, following a twenty-five-year career as a police officer. While in the police department, Huey had also served in the Air Force Reserves, where he was classified as a behavioral science specialist. He had earned a bachelor's degree in criminal justice and a master's degree in counseling. Between his work as a police officer, counselor in the military, and child abuse investigator, Huey had seen hundreds of families and a full range of abuse and dysfunction. Although he had not received much in the way of formal training about child abuse and neglect, he was sure he had the "street smarts" and experience to be a skilled investigator.

Directly after he was assigned the case, Huey went to the hospital to observe Marie and read her medical chart. He talked with the medical staff, met both parents at the hospital, and reviewed the Physician's Report of Examination, which would serve as the basis for the court petition to be filed that same day. Huey also arranged to make a home visit to talk with the parents about Marie and her injuries.

Once Marie's case was assigned to the CANTS unit for investigation, it proceeded in an appropriate fashion. Although Dr. Systram had not fulfilled her role as a sentinel, the other sentinels in the hospital emergency room and the CANTS unit did work seamlessly to protect Marie.

Home Visits

Huey arranged to visit Darlene and Donald Edwards in their apartment in the early evening of May 27. Donald worked late and came home about an hour after Huey had arrived at the apartment. Huey had already talked with Darlene about the process and purpose of his investigation and had looked around the apartment. The normal procedures for a child abuse investigation required the investigator to make careful note of the household environment, including checking the refrigerator and cabinets for food supplies, and looking at the child's sleeping and living arrangements.

Huey's observations of the Edwards home were not particularly remarkable. He described the Edwardses as "average young America." There was a separate room for the baby, with a crib, baby furniture, toys, sufficient clothing, and boxes of disposable diapers stacked up in the corner of the room. The rest of the apartment was neat and well-kept. Huey went so far as to check out the family car and found that a baby seat was buckled properly in the back.

Neither parent could seem to account for Marie's injuries. Donald said he worked long hours and that Darlene was responsible for caring for the baby. Darlene also could not explain how Marie had been injured. After a ninety-minute interview, Huey was no closer to determining the cause of injury than when he began. He felt that each parent suspected the other, which led him to the preliminary conclusion that one parent had inflicted the injury—he just could not determine which one it was.

Later that evening, Huey drove out to the suburbs to interview Marie's maternal grandparents, both to learn more about Darlene's background and to see whether they could have inflicted the injuries while baby-sitting Marie. The grandparents reported that they had cared for Marie the weekend before she was injured. Darlene's stepfather said he had noticed a small bruise on the back of Marie's neck. He also remembered that when Marie was fed on Saturday she immediately started to vomit.

Huey had no doubt that Donald or Darlene had inflicted the injury. But significantly, had the injury been less severe or had Donald and Darlene offered a better explanation for it, it is possible Huey would not have "substantiated" or "founded" the case.[1]

Substantiating a Case

One week after Marie was admitted to the hospital, Albert Huey finished his investigation of her case and also filed a report with the city police department. He didn't expect much to come of the report to the police. First, in the absence of a statement by either parent against the other, there was little on which to base a criminal charge. Second, nonfatal child abuse is almost always considered the province of child welfare agencies. The enactment of the reporting laws in the 1960s essentially decriminalized child maltreatment—with the exception of homicides. Thus child welfare agencies bear almost the complete responsibility for investigating child abuse—even though the attack on Marie was legally a case of felonious assault and battery.

Filing for Custody

The next day, May 31, Huey assembled his notes and files from his four-day investigation into the injuries sustained by Marie Edwards and met with one of the lawyers in the DCF office of legal affairs. Huey and the attorney reviewed Huey's files, including the Physician's Report of Examination. They also discussed Huey's interviews with Darlene and Donald Edwards, Darlene's mother and stepfather, and Dr. Systram. The seriousness of the injuries, and the fact that there was no reasonable explanation for them other than an assault by either or both parents, governed Huey and the attorney's thinking about what to do with the case. They decided to file immediately with Family Court to have Marie's legal and physical custody continued with the state. Under this action, Marie would not go home with her parents when she was released from the hospital and she would not be reunited with them until a court hearing was held to determine whether they were fit to have Marie returned to them.

The most notable feature of the case of Marie Edwards occurred at this point. At the age of six weeks, she had suffered a life-threatening injury that would ultimately prove to disable her for the rest of her life. Although her injury and risk were so significant that there was no thought of immediately returning her to her parents, the case plan called for reunification, as mandated by a federal law (the Adoption Assistance and Child Welfare Act of 1980, PL 96-272) that requires states to make "reasonable efforts" to keep or reunite children with their birth parents. This policy is discussed in detail in chapter 4.

The Assessment Worker

Marie Edwards was still hospitalized a week later, June 6, when her case was reassigned from CANTS investigator Huey to an assessment worker, Lisa Hanratty. Hanratty had been with the Department of Children and Their Families six and a half years: a year and a half as a Direct Services worker and five years in assessment. With a bachelor's degree in psychology and a master's in social work, she was far better educated than most employees who carry out child abuse and neglect assessments. In addition, she was experienced in both assessment and the availability of direct services. Finally, because Hanratty was an assessment worker, her caseload was low: an average of eight or nine cases, compared to the thirty to forty families she carried when she was a Direct Services worker. The light caseload was purposefully set by the agency administration to allow for intensive and vigilant efforts to assess families and their needs.

Hanratty collected the case file and left the office to make an unannounced visit to the Edwards home. Such visits are carried out on occasion to observe families in their so-called natural state—giving them no time to clean the house or rehearse.

Darlene Edwards was home alone when Hanratty arrived.

Hanratty had not bothered to consult with Albert Huey about the case, and had not yet reviewed his notes about it. Had she read the file or talked with Huey, she would have noticed that the Edwards apartment was still as neat and organized as it had been when Huey had made his own scheduled home visit a little more than a week earlier. Boxes of diapers and a pile of clothing were still neatly stacked in the baby's room.

Hanratty noted that Darlene Edwards seemed depressed: her affect was flat and she spoke in a monotone. Hanratty pursued a general line of questioning and then began to focus on Marie's injuries and how they might have occurred. Darlene answered simply, "I don't know." She gave little impression that she either knew or even cared how her daughter had been hurt. Hanratty turned the line of questioning to the issue of when Marie could be returned home. Hanratty's goal, as dictated by the policy of "reasonable efforts," was to learn what psychological and social interventions Darlene would be amenable to as a condition of being reunited with her daughter. Darlene continued to answer in monosyllables and showed no eagerness or even interest in having Marie come home right away. In fact, it seemed that Marie's being out of the house seemed to lessen Darlene's feelings of being overwhelmed. But her reluctance to have her daughter come home was given little weight by Hanratty, her supervisor, or the department. Their goal in this and all cases was to develop a reunification case plan.

The day after Hanratty visited Darlene, she and one of the department lawyers, Dan O'Brien, were in family court for a probable-cause hearing on the Marie Edwards case. The court had reviewed the documents provided by the Department of Children and Their Families and had considered the parents' plea of not guilty. The medical evidence regarding Marie's injuries and the parents' lack of a convincing or even credible explanation for them were sufficient grounds for the judge to continue Marie's physical and legal custody with the department. Hanratty left family court with two tasks. First she had to find a home for Marie to go to when she was discharged from the hospital. Second, she had to continue her assessment of the family, identify appropriate services for them, and develop a plan for reuniting Marie with her parents.

The Investigation of David's Case

When David was born, the Edwards family was an "open case" for the Department of Children and Their Families. The open case was Marie, who was still in a foster home; the Edwardses (as described in the next chapter) were still involved with a DCF Direct Services worker, Karen Hastings.

Karen Hastings was aware of the birth of David, as she had been assigned to Marie's case in July 1988, just before he was born. Hastings had seen David on a couple of occasions, mostly while supervising visits between Donald, Darlene, and Marie. Hastings apparently took little notice of David. Her main focus was whether Marie would be returned to Donald and Darlene or whether the department would seek to terminate their parental rights—but only the rights to Marie. David, in the eyes of Karen Hastings, existed only on the very fringes of the case.

The case of Marie Edwards was closed by the Department

of Children and Their Families September 27, 1989, when Donald and Darlene voluntarily terminated their parental rights to her. From this date until April 23, 1990, when the department responded to the first anonymous call about David, there were no home visits, no follow-up, nor any monitoring of David Edwards.

The case of David Edwards was assigned to Justine Peters three days later after the anonymous call was received. The report on David was given the lowest priority. First, the nature of the reported condition—pale and skinny and a previous vague injury to his elbow—did not suggest that he was in imminent danger. Second, the source of the report, an anonymous caller, typically is considered the least reliable source by those in the child welfare system. Thus David Edwards ended up at the bottom of the CANTS triage.

Justine Peters, who had a bachelor's degree in social work, had been an investigator in the Department of Children and Their Families for two years when she was assigned David's case. Her first action was to check to see whether the Edwardses were either an open or prior case in the department. When Peters learned that the family had been an active case, she consulted with Madeline Rauch, Karen Hastings's supervisor, who informed her that the Edwardses had reluctantly signed a voluntary termination of parental rights on their daughter Marie seven months earlier. Rauch also noted that the parents had been seen by a clinician at a local mental health center, that the case file suggested some marijuana use in the home, and that the parents would likely be angry and verbally threatening.

This meeting and a cursory review of Marie's case was the

sum total of information Justine Peters took with her into the investigation of the CANTS report on David Edwards. Peters did not examine Marie's file because, as she explained at a hearing on David's death, she hadn't wanted "any information to interfere with an objective investigation." This decision, which Peters's supervisor did not overrule, was a critical mistake, since it left out the single most important item in the risk assessment: past behavior.

A Scheduled Visit

Justine Peters called the Edwards home to tell Darlene a child maltreatment report had been received on David and to schedule a home visit for the same day.

Only Darlene and David were at home when Peters visited—Donald was at work. Peters explained the reason for her visit to Darlene, toured the apartment, and asked to look David over. He did not appear too pale or skinny to Peters. He did have a small bruise on his forehead, which Darlene said happened when he fell on a toy in his crib. The apartment was as neat as it had been when Albert Huey had visited it nearly two years earlier. Darlene Edwards was neither angry nor belligerent, much to Peters's relief.

The Medical Inquiry

The next day, Justine Peters called Dr. Tanner to discuss the allegation that David Edwards had been maltreated. Dr. Tanner reported that she had been "very concerned" about

David's fluctuating weight and his bruises. Tanner also said Darlene was showing signs of postpartum depression. Peters asked Dr. Tanner whether she would diagnose David as a failure-to-thrive baby. Tanner said no. She repeated that she had concerns about the child's lack of weight gain and, as a result, had scheduled appointments at intervals shorter than usual to monitor his weight. Peters concluded that the doctor was not saying David was at risk or should be removed from the home. Peters never informed Dr. Tanner about the case of Marie Edwards, so the doctor remained unaware of the history of serious abuse in the Edwards home.

Having checked out the possibility of failure to thrive, Peters next tried to look into the matter of the chipped elbow. The day after her conversation with Dr. Tanner, Peters contacted the hospital—the same hospital that had treated Marie Edwards and where Darlene had visited a social worker to discuss her depression. Phone calls to the emergency room, pediatric social worker, and other staff turned up no records of a chipped elbow. David had been treated in November 1989 for an elbow injury, but the emergency room chart was vague about the nature of the injury and there was no available X-ray of David's arm.[2]

An Unannounced Visit

Peters made an unannounced visit to the Edwards home April 26, three days after her first visit, and timed it so that there would be a good chance both Donald and Darlene Edwards would be at home. Peters seemed to detect the acrid smell of marijuana when she entered the Edwardses' apartment. Only Darlene and David were at home, and Peters confronted her about the marijuana smell. Darlene shot back, "You can't prove nothing," and the line of questioning ended there.

Peters asked Darlene about the so-called chipped elbow. Darlene answered that David had indeed hurt his elbow in November, when the Edwardses were visiting a friend's house and David had apparently fallen against a piece of furniture. Darlene said that David had been treated by an orthopedic surgeon and that the elbow was neither "broken nor fractured." Darlene's explanation was not plausible, since the then four-month-old David would not have been mobile enough to "fall" against a piece of furniture. Peters took note of the inconsistency, but could do little with it since she had no X-ray or medical report to confirm that the elbow was actually injured.

Donald came home about a half hour after Peters's arrival. Up until this time, Darlene had been generally cooperative and had answered all of Peters's questions—except for the one about marijuana. Darlene's demeanor changed immediately when Donald arrived. She became angrier. Donald was outright belligerent, defiant, and rude, according to Peters's report. Donald's response to most of Peters's questions was, "You're not taking the kid—you're not taking *this* kid!"

Peters re-examined David. This time she asked Darlene to remove all of his clothes, even his diaper. Peters checked for bruises and diaper rash. David had no bruises besides the one on his forehead that Peters had observed three days earlier.

Darlene again said that David had bumped his head on a toy in his crib. Peters accepted this explanation and marked it as "feasible" in her notes on the visit.

Peters broached the subject of marijuana one more time. She asked Donald whether Darlene used drugs. He responded, "I don't know if she uses drugs or smokes pot." Darlene again strenuously denied using marijuana or any other kind of drugs.

This unannounced home visit was the final step in the risk assessment. Peters did make one more attempt to contact an orthopedic surgeon at the hospital to track down the chipped elbow event, but again came up with nothing.

Based on her two home visits, her interview with Dr. Tanner, and the hospital records on David, Justine Peters concluded that David was receiving adequate home and medical care. However, given the history of injury to Marie and the subsequent voluntary termination of parental rights to her, and given Dr. Tanner's concern about David's lack of weight gain, Peters concluded that this was a "valid" report of "other neglect."

Peters recommended that the case be turned over to the Screening and Assessment Unit, that Darlene and Donald be steered toward parental counseling, that an assessment of parental substance abuse be made, and that David be referred to the "Early Start" educational enrichment program, a state-run program similar to the federal Head Start program, but for younger children. Although Peters felt that the family was in need of support services, she did not believe David should be taken away from his parents. She did not consult with the department legal staff, nor did she talk to her supervisor about the possibility of changing the legal or physical custody of David Edwards. David, she felt, would be safe in the home.

A Second Assessment

Five days later, the case of David Edwards was assigned to Pauline Mitchell, an assessment worker who had been on the job less than a month. Mitchell, who had a bachelor's degree in elementary education, had previously worked with mentally retarded adults before taking the civil service test to become an assessment worker. She went through about two weeks of training—although the actual classroom time was twenty hours. Two weeks after her training ended, she had a caseload of seven families to assess. David Edwards was her eighth case.

Mitchell too familiarized herself with the Edwards family case file. She too found out about Marie and the termination of parental rights.

Pauline Mitchell made four home visits, on May 8, 10, 24, and 31. She also interviewed Dr. Tanner and pursued the matter of the chipped elbow, but she too could not find an X-ray, physician, or medical records that provided anything more than the vaguest account of the November elbow injury.

Darlene and Donald Edwards's anger was much greater with Pauline Mitchell than with investigator Justine Peters. Neither parent was willing to discuss the case at length and Donald grew more hostile with each visit. He did, however, agree to sign medical release forms so that Mitchell could discuss the case with Dr. Tanner and obtain David's medical records from her and the hospital.

Darlene did volunteer that she had decided not to continue to use Alice Tanner as David's pediatrician. In the six months between his last visit to Dr. Tanner and his death, David was not seen by any physician.

After the four home visits, Mitchell recommended that the family be involved in some kind of home nursing, at least once a week. This would provide some monitoring of David's weight and give Darlene some help with feeding him and meeting his needs. Mitchell also picked up on Darlene's depression and her sense of being trapped and recommended "other" services, including some kind of baby-sitting so Darlene could have some time to herself.

The services were never delivered. According to Mitchell, Donald Edwards called to tell her that he wanted the department to get out of his life and to keep its spies out of his home. Darlene, however, did agree to see a social worker at the hospital again to discuss her feelings of being "overwhelmed."

On June 5, the CANTS line received the second anonymous call about David Edwards, the one that said he was "failing." The report was referred to Pauline Mitchell, who did not seem overly concerned about it; she had just seen David on May 31 and he seemed fine, and she had already planned an unannounced visit for June 7.

When Mitchell arrived, Darlene was at home with David, who crawled and played during the visit and showed no visible signs of "failure" and no visible injuries. Mitchell did not examine him during this visit, other than just watching him play on the floor.

Later that afternoon Donald Edwards called Mitchell to express his outrage that the department was still "harassing" him, his wife, and his son. Edwards declared that he would not allow anyone from the department back into his home without a warrant.

Twelve days later, Pauline Mitchell decided to try to schedule one more visit to the Edwards home. She was not really interested in observing David again; rather, her goal was to convince Darlene and Donald to accept the services she was recommending: home nurse visits and parental counseling. Donald agreed to the visit.

Resistance to Offers of Help

Donald was able to control his emotions during this visit. He did, however, refuse to accept any of Mitchell's recommendations, insisting he did not want any more services from DCF and that if DCF wanted to do something, they'd better have a court order to do it.

Finally, before she left the Edwards home for the last time, Mitchell decided to take one more look at David. She asked whether she could pick him up and examine him. Darlene sighed and said yes. Mitchell, a bit apprehensive that Donald might become angry if she overstayed her welcome, picked David up. He turned toward her face and smiled. Later, at the postmortem hearing, Mitchell would describe the child's bright smile and then break down in tears.

In the end, Mitchell had concerns about David, but believed she had little hard evidence to indicate that he was at risk. In her final report, she seemingly agreed with Donald that the case should be about David and not about Marie. At the postmortem hearing, Mitchell would testify:

> I looked at the family history as part of my assessment. In terms of legal action, I really didn't have any idea about what could be done with that. I did not at all disregard what had happened with the daughter, but I can't speculate on what would have happened to the infant son in the future because of what happened to the daughter.

The flaw in Mitchell's conclusion is that she, like Justine Peters before her, had deliberately ignored the single most important risk factor in the case, the previous abuse of Marie. She most certainly could have and should have speculated about what might happen to David based on what did happen to Marie. Mitchell did not apply a basic maxim of psychology: The best way to predict what someone will do tomorrow is to know what he or she did yesterday.

Why did Mitchell fail to see the risk facing David Edwards? Part of the answer is that the child welfare system's overriding goal of family preservation creates a blind spot in the process of risk assessment. Prior history is given less weight than it deserves because child welfare agencies see their goal as keeping children with their biological parents. If child safety were the main goal, a history of harm to other children would play a more important part in the risk assessment process.

Legal Opinion

After her last visit to the Edwards home, Mitchell consulted on two occasions with two department lawyers. Both told her she had no legal grounds to petition family court for a change of legal and/or physical custody of David. In their opinion, there simply was no clear and convincing evidence that David had been maltreated or was at risk of being maltreated in the future.

They were wrong. There was legal precedent in the state to use prior abuse of another child as a basis for seeking custody or even terminating parental rights. The department could have sought legal custody of David based on the reports that he was neglected and the prior abuse of Marie. Here again, the overriding concern with family preservation prevented the department from taking advantage of their legal ability to protect a child reported for abuse and neglect.

Finally, Mitchell met with her supervisor, Joan Rothman, whose recommendation was short and to the point: Close the case; there's nothing more to be done. Rothman's reading of the record was that no evidence of abuse or neglect had been uncovered but that there *was* evidence of "bonding" between the parents and the child.

Had Mitchell wanted to appeal this recommendation or those of the lawyers, she could have gone to the department's chief legal counsel and asked him to file a petition in family court. Mitchell, however, decided to follow her supervisor's and the lawyers' recommendations and close the case.

On July 2, 1990, Mitchell called Donald Edwards and told

him that, based on her assessment, the Department of Children and Their Families had decided to close the case. There would be no legal action or further involvement by DCF.

Three and a half months later, David Edwards would arrive in the emergency room dead on arrival.

CAN WE PREDICT AND PREVENT?

Could the fatal abuse of David have been predicted? Could his death have been prevented? If our goal is to create a safe world for children, one central question is how can we better assess risk, predict abuse, and prevent injury and death?

Let's pretend we have a risk assessment instrument that is 99 percent accurate—that is, it will accurately predict the risk of fatal, serious, and moderate abuse in 99 of 100 cases. Of course, no such instrument exists.

To prevent abuse before it occurs, we would use our risk assessment instrument to screen the entire population of American children under the age of eighteen—about 63 million children.

The National Center on Child Abuse and Neglect estimates that 900,000 children are at risk of serious or moderate physical abuse each year.[3] Given a 99 percent accurate risk assessment, we will identify 99 percent of this total and miss 1 percent, or 9,000 children. Thus, there will be 9,000 false negative assessments.

There is also a 1 percent risk of false positives. Thus, 1 percent of all children screened (63 million), or 630,000 children screened, will be false positive assessments. Clearly, children could be protected by a system of population-wide risk assessment, but the problem of false positives is too great to overcome even with the most accurate risk assessment instrument.

Who Should Be Screened?

The only feasible approach to reduce false positives is to limit the size of the population that is screened. The obvious group that can and does receive risk assessment are the 3 million cases of suspected child maltreatment reported annually. These cases are screened and assessed. Yet even these assessments often fail to identify risk, as in the case of David Edwards. How can risk assessment be improved?

Identifying Risk

Risk assessment is a formalized method that provides a uniform structure and criteria for determining risk.[4] A survey conducted in 1991 found that forty-two of the fifty states have experimented with or implemented some form of systematic risk assessment.[5]

In evaluating both Marie and David Edwards, the Department of Children and Their Families used a type of risk assessment form known as a "matrix" approach.[6] The form requires an investigator like Pauline Mitchell to identify specific child, caretaker, and environmental factors and derive a "risk score." The factors assessed are presented in table 3.1.

Table 3.1
Assessment of Risk Summary Factor Index

Factors	Low Risk 1	2	Intermediate Risk 3	4	High Risk 5	Point
CHILD FACTORS						
1A. Child's age	Adolescent, secondary-school age	Upper elementary-school age	Lower elementary-school age	Preschool	Infant	
1B. Child's physical/mental abilities	Cares for and protects self without adult assistance (0%)	Requires a minimal amount of assistance to care and protect self (25%)	Requires adult assistance to care for and protect self (50%)	Unable to care for and protect self without substantial adult assistance (75%)	Completely unable to care for and protect self without adult assistance (100%)	
CARETAKER FACTORS						
2A. Caretaker's level of cooperation	Aware of problem, works with social service agency to resolve problem	Not aware of problem but works with social service agency to protect child	Overly compliant with investigator	Hostile, but will work with social service agency as a result of police action or court order	Doesn't believe there is a problem, refuses to cooperate	
2B. Caretaker's physical, emotional abilities/control	Realistic expectation of child, can plan to correct problem	Unsure how to protect child, but able to assist in planning	Poor reasoning abilities, may be physically handicapped, needs planning assistance to protect child	Unable to control anger or impulses	Poor conception of reality or severe mental or physical impairment	
2C. Caretaker alcohol/substance abuse	Not suspected of substance abuse	Successfully completed treatment program	Known user, in treatment program	Suspected user, not in treatment	Known user, resistant to treatment	

Table 3.1 (*cont.*)
Assessment of Risk Summary Factor Index

Factors	Low Risk 1	2	Intermediate Risk 3	4	High Risk 5	Point
PERPETRATOR FACTORS						
3A. Rationality of perpetrator's behavior	Accidental injury, adequate supervision (rational)	Accidental injury, lack of supervision	Minor injury resulting from excessive corporal discipline	Inappropriate weapon used to harm child	Injury the result of desire to permanently harm child (irrational)	
3B. Perpetrator's access to child	Out of home, no access to child	Out of home, difficult access to child	In home, access to child is difficult	Out of home, easy access to child	In home, complete access to child	
INCIDENT FACTORS						
4A. Extent of permanent harm	Abuse/neglect has no discernible effect on child	Abuse/neglect limits child's participation in normal social activity	Abuse/neglect results in physical injury discomfort, no medical attention needed	Abuse/neglect produces readily observable permanent injury	Abuse/neglect results in death or permanent dysfunction of an organ or limb	
4B. Location of injury	Bony body parts, knees, elbows, buttocks	Extremities, fleshy parts of arms and legs	Torso	Internal injury	Head, face, and genitals	
4C. Previous history of abuse/neglect	No previous reported history of abuse/neglect	Previous abuse/neglect of siblings, not Priority 1 allegations	Previous abuse/neglect of child, not Priority 1	Previous abuse/neglect of siblings, Priority 1 allegations	Previous abuse/neglect of child, Priority 1 allegations	

Table 3.1 (*cont.*)
Assessment of Risk Summary Factor Index

Factors	Low Risk 1	2	Intermediate Risk 3	4	High Risk 5	Point
4D. Physical condition of home	Home is clean with no apparent safety or health hazards	Dirty home, some accumulated garbage, generally cluttered and unkept	Trash and garbage not disposed, animal (pet) droppings in home, mold growing on dirty dishes	Unsound steps, exposed wiring, urine-soaked mattresses	Structurally unsound, leaky roof and windows, walls bending under weight, holes in exterior walls	
ENVIRONMENTAL FACTORS						
5A. External support	Family, neighbors, and friends available; good community resources	Limited community resources; family and friends available	Family supportive but not in geographic area; some support from friends	Little support from family or friends; no community resources	Caretaker/family has no relatives or friends and is geographically isolated from community services	
5B. Stress	Stable family, steady employment, nonmobile	Trouble at work, change of residence	Birth of child	Incarceration of family member, or divorce	Death of spouse	
5C. Family mobility	No moves past two years	Moved once in past year	Moved twice in past two years	Moved three times in past two years	Moved more than three times in past two years	
					TOTAL Enter total for child on CANTS 2 (J6)	

There are a number of problems with the form used by DCF and many other agencies. First, and perhaps foremost, investigators, assessment workers, and other personnel who use the form get little training in how to use it; as a result, they fail to see how the form connects to the actual knowledge base on what factors are known to raise the risk for severe or fatal abuse of children. Second, the form treats every item as being of equal importance. Risk is determined by a summary score. Thus the fact that a parent has previously fractured the skull of her first child is given equal weight with the existence of an alcohol or substance abuse problem. The former is a prominent risk factor, while the latter is the subject of debate as a risk factor for serious child abuse.[7] Third, some factors on the form are known to be *un*related to the risk of severe or fatal child abuse: for example, factor 4D, "Physical condition of home." During postmortem interviews, both Albert Huey and Pauline Mitchell made a point of how neat, clean, and well stocked Edwardses' apartment was.

Child protection workers have for years used what I call "olfactory risk assessment" when conducting home visits. Homes that reek of urine or feces, that are strewn with trash and garbage, are typically rated as high-risk, even in the absence of other risk factors. Similarly, homes that smell of cleanser and are neat as a pin are regarded as low-risk, even when other important risk factors are present.

Without training in how to weight risk factors and how to use a risk assessment instrument properly, investigators often apply the instrument subjectively. Or, in the words of Albert Huey, "We develop a clinical impression of what is the level of risk, come up with a total risk assessment score that reflects that assessment, and then go back and fill in the boxes so that they total up to our clinical impression."

Through three decades of research on child abuse and neglect, through the many more decades of research on violent and aggressive human behavior, and through all the accumulated social scientific research on human behavior, one factor stands out as the best possible predictor of future behavior: past behavior. Obviously, people do change, and past behavior is not a *perfect* predictor of what someone will do in the future. But of all the factors considered in a risk assessment, the one that is most likely to predict future risk is how parents have treated their children in the past. The fact that either Donald or Darlene inflicted a grievous injury on six-week-old Marie should have been a huge warning flag in the assessment of David Edwards. Moreover, the parents', especially Darlene's, failure to comply with the demands of the department in order to regain custody of Marie should also have been a warning about the possible dangers that awaited David.

A second factor that should have stood out in any risk assessment was the fact that the department had made no meaningful or effective intervention with the parents between the time of the first child's injury and the birth of the second child. Pauline Mitchell, during an interview after David's death, said she had thought things would be better for David because he was a boy and Donald might feel closer to or more protective of him. Mitchell also speculated that having had their first child taken away might have "sent a message" to Donald and Darlene to be more careful with their new baby.

Neither supposition is firmly grounded in any research on child abuse and neglect or the process that people go through when they change their behaviors. At best, these conjectures were wishful thinking.

Research on predicting severe child abuse and neglect suggests other important risk factors that should be considered in any risk assessment.[8]

Age of child: Perhaps the most consistent finding in the child abuse and neglect literature is that babies under one year of age are at the greatest risk of being injured or killed by their parents or other caretakers, and that toddlers ages one to three are the next-highest risk group. While there is some debate as to whether this is due to infants being more fragile and more vulnerable to injury, parents having a more difficult time meeting their needs than those of older children, or simply younger children having younger parents, there is little dispute among researchers or child protection workers about the greater vulnerability of infants and toddlers.

Age of caretaker: Young caretakers are also more likely to severely injure or kill their children than older caretakers are. This may be because of immaturity, a greater likelihood of having a young child, or a greater likelihood of having low income or low socioeconomic status.

Sex of child: Whether boys or girls are more likely to be killed or abused is less clear than the age factor. Although the survey and clinical data are far from conclusive, it appears that boys are slightly more likely to be injured or killed compared to girls.

Sex of caretaker: Mothers, because they spend more time

with their children and have a greater responsibility for child care, are more likely to use physical discipline than fathers are. But males, although they spend less time with children and have less overall responsibility for child care, are more likely than females to injure or kill children. The Edwards family was an exception: It was David's mother who ultimately confessed to killing him, and most of the child welfare personnel who worked with the family suspected that it was she who injured Marie.

Women who severely injure or kill children are typically closely related to the victim: A child's mother is more likely to kill or injure him than his stepmother is. Male offenders tend to be more distantly related to their victims: A child's stepfather or the boyfriend of his mother is more likely to kill or injure him than his father is.

Social factors: Although researchers have consistently found that child abuse is more likely to occur in lower-income homes than in richer ones,[9] income, education, and occupation of the caretakers are not adequate or accurate predictors of severe or fatal abuse. As noted previously, a messy, smelly, and disorganized home may be a sign of possible neglect, but it is essentially unrelated to the risk of severe or fatal abuse.

Parents' status as child abuse victims: If TV talk shows and documentaries are to be believed, the single best predictor of severe abuse is whether a caretaker was abused as a child. For example, in the widely acclaimed documentary *Scared Silent,* narrated by Oprah Winfrey and broadcast on all three commercial television networks and the Public Broadcasting Service over Labor Day weekend 1992, *all* the perpetrators of abuse who were interviewed had been victims of abuse themselves. And, indeed, retrospective studies of child maltreatment find that as many as 90 percent of identified offenders were abused as children.[10] Looking at abuse prospectively, however, only about 30 percent of those who were abused grow up to be abusive caretakers. Thus while the majority of abusive parents were abused, only a minority of those who were abused ever become abusers; therefore, a parent's status as an abuse victim is a weak predictive factor. Moreover, even if it were a strong predictor, it is much more difficult to measure accurately than the other risk factors we have reviewed. If parents know that their history of being abused is considered a risk factor, we would assume they would try to conceal it from an investigator. For example, neither Donald nor Darlene Edwards was forthcoming about whether they were abused or neglected by their parents. After David's death, it became clearer that Darlene had probably been sexually abused as a child by one of her mother's boyfriends.

Substance abuse: Conventional wisdom holds that alcohol use and abuse is a major risk factor for violent behavior in general and family violence in particular. The "demon rum" explanation is one of the most pervasive and widely believed explanations for family violence in the professional and popular literature. Illicit drugs, such as cocaine, heroin, marijuana, and LSD, are also considered causal agents in child abuse, spouse abuse, and other forms of family violence. That alcohol and substance abuse may be related to, or directly cause, family violence is not a new idea. William Hogarth's etching "Gin Lane," done in the early 1700s, graphically portrays the misery that befalls children whose parents abuse alcohol.[11] Social workers in the United States in the 1800s believed alcohol was the cause of child abuse, and the Prohibition movement in the United States in the 1910s was partially based on the assumption that drinking led to the mistreatment of children.[12]

The argument that alcohol causes violent behavior is based on the proposition that alcohol is a "superego solvent," reducing inhibitions and allowing violent behavior to emerge. Cocaine, heroin, LSD, and marijuana have also been postulated as direct causal agents that reduce inhibitions and unleash violent tendencies.

Common sense and conventional wisdom notwithstanding, there is little scientific evidence to support the claim that alcohol and drugs (with the exception of amphetamines and steroids), have chemical and pharmacological properties that directly produce violent and abusive behavior. Evidence from cross-cultural research, laboratory studies, blood tests of men arrested for wife-beating, and surveys all indicate that while alcohol use may be *associated with* family violence, it is not a primary *cause* of it.[13]

Although alcohol and most drugs are not direct causal agents in acts of violence, they can be considered risk factors under certain conditions. The amount of alcohol consumed by a caretaker may not, in and of itself, be a risk factor for serious or fatal abuse. In fact, research finds that the heaviest drinkers are not the likeliest to commit serious violence.[14] Those who are binge drinkers are. Similarly, although drugs do not *cause* violent behavior, use of controlled substances is *related* to the likelihood of severe violence toward children.

The risk assessment form used by Pauline Mitchell in the

David Edwards case asks whether substance abuse is suspected, whether the caretaker has successfully completed a treatment program or is in one, or is a known user who is resistant to treatment. Aside from the fact that these are often going to be subjective judgments, especially in the case of classifying someone as "resistant to treatment," the classification categories on the form are not actually related to increased risk for serious or fatal abuse.

Social isolation: Abusers in general, and serious abusers in particular, are known to have few friends, limited contact with neighbors, few close relatives they live near and/or are in contact with, and few memberships or affiliations in community groups. In the vast majority of cases of fatal abuse, when neighbors are questioned they have little to report. They might mention that the individual or couple were having marital problems, or that fights and yelling could be heard. But almost without exception, neighbors report that they knew little about the family. In many cases the abuser has lived in the community for less than a year.

In addition to being socially isolated, offenders are highly resistant to intervention. Although serious abusers may be forced to join psychological or substance abuse treatment programs, they are the most likely to drop out of them.[15]

The assessment form identifies these risk factors in two items: 5A, "External support," and 5C, "Family mobility." However, the form provides few guidelines for the investigator in assessing external support, and the categories for family mobility omit the highest-risk category: lived in the community for one year or less.

Stress: It has been axiomatic for nearly three decades that certain stressful events and a pileup of stressful events are central risk factors for child abuse. Unemployment; physical or mental illness; death of a close relative or close friend; sexual difficulties; environmental stressors; and the birth of a new baby do raise the risk for abuse. However, these stressors become much more important if they occur in a family that has limited financial, social, or psychological resources.

The assessment form would have classified the Edwards family at the midpoint of risk for factor 5B, "Stress," because of the birth of David. The Edwardses would not have been classified at the high end of risk because they did not have a family member incarcerated, had not divorced, and neither spouse had died. It is in the measurement of stress that this particular assessment form is the most inadequate and inaccurate. Although "death of a spouse" would normally be given a high value as a family stressor, it is an inappropriate item to be given the highest. First, the death of a spouse is an extremely rare event in the lives of those at highest risk for abusing their children: young parents.[16] Second, other risk factors, especially unemployment, are more likely to occur and are better predictors of serious abuse.

COMBINING RISK FACTORS: MODELS OF CHILD ABUSE

No behavior as complex as child maltreatment can be explained by any one risk factor or even a list of factors such as those listed in the previous section. That is why social scientists develop models to explain child abuse. Yet after the rediscovery of child abuse in the 1960s, the model of child maltreatment was a single-factor model—psychopathology or mental illness was why parents abused their children. It followed that the best way to protect maltreated children was to remove them from their "sick" parents and attempt to rehabilitate the abusers, typically through psychiatric treatment or counseling.

One of the first social scientists to challenge the mental-illness explanation of child abuse, David Gil, found convincing evidence that social factors, such as poverty, unemployment, social isolation, and marital conflict, were strongly related to the risk of abuse.[17] Although most poor parents do not abuse their children and abuse can be found in all social classes and at all income levels, cases of child abuse and neglect do occur disproportionately in lower-class, lower-income families.

Social scientists began to find convincing evidence that only a small portion of child abusers—about 10 percent—could be diagnosed as either suffering from mental illness or psychopathology. Social factors were thought to account for the other 90 percent.[18] Even the psychiatrist Brandt Steele, one of the early proponents of the psychopathological explanation of abuse, came to agree with these estimates in the late 1970s.[19]

Anyone Can Abuse: The Continuum Model

The quality of the research on child abuse and neglect improved in the 1970s and 1980s. Small, nonrepresentative sample studies that lacked control groups were replaced with larger studies using statistical analyses based on official reports or social surveys.[20]

The new theories proposed that "anyone" could abuse his or her child in certain circumstances: when the stresses on them outweighed the supports they had.[21] This *continuum model* rejected the psychiatric or psychological "kind of person" explanation for maltreatment. Abusers and neglectors were not defective, deviant, or sick individuals; rather, they experienced what I called a "tipping point," when social stresses and/or child-produced stressors such as colic, developmental delays, or delinquency piled up, pushing parents over the edge from being caring to abusive. According to this model, a parent who fractured her child's skull was not much different from one who couldn't keep house.

I also proposed a *deficit model* of parental behavior. It assumes that some people lack the personal, social, and economic resources to be effective parents. Offering resources, such as psychological counseling, parent education, or home visitors, would help parents to meet their own needs and the needs of their children. I argued that the proper goal of child welfare interventions was to add resources, remove stresses, or both, thus making the home safe again so that abused children could be reunited with their parents.

Is Everyone Really a Potential Abuser?

In 1986 my colleague Ake Edfeldt and I compared the rates of violence toward children in the United States and in Sweden. We found that the rate of physical punishment of children was significantly lower in Sweden; however, the rate of *severe* (or abusive) violence was the same in both countries. Explaining the similarity in the rate of severe violence, we stated:

> [K]icking, biting, punching, beating, and using weapons could be considered either more expressive forms of violence . . . or forms of violence consciously designed to inflict serious injury on a child. These behaviors may be less amenable to control by imposing a cultural standard that spanking is wrong.[22]

Equally plausible, however, is that physical punishment and severe violence are *distinct* forms of behavior, attributable to distinct causes.

A 1987 analysis of homicide rates found different generative causes for different types of violence. The researcher discovered that the set of sociocultural factors that explain almost all state-to-state differences in adult homicide rates, such as poverty and pre-existing social relationships, does not explain differences among states' homicide deaths of infants.[23]

Figures 3.1–3.3 illustrate three different assumptions about child abuse and neglect. The continuum model, represented in figure 3.1, suggests that parents can range from lovingly meeting all their children's developmental and physical needs, to torturing, maiming, and deliberately killing their children.

Figure 3.2 represents the plausible but highly unlikely notion that there are distinct types of abusers with no overlap

Figure 3.1
The Continuum Model of Parental Violence and Child Abuse

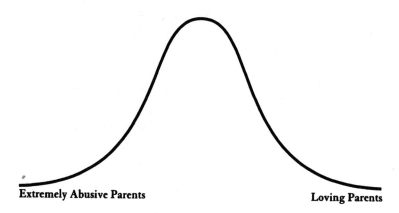

Extremely Abusive Parents　　　　　　　　**Loving Parents**

between the types. This greatly oversimplified figure is a version of the model of human behavior Woody Allen presented in his movie *Annie Hall,* where he divides the world into the "horrible" and the "miserable." In figure 3.2 the horrible are parents who deliberately kill or torture their children. In the words of Woody Allen, the miserable are "everyone else."

Figure 3.2
Two Distinct Types of Abusers

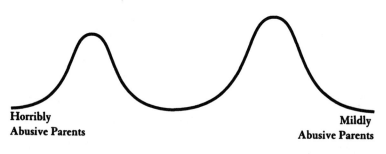

Horribly
Abusive Parents　　　　　　　　**Mildly**
　　　　　　　　　　　　　　　　Abusive Parents

Figure 3.3 presents a more realistic model, which proposes distinct types of abusers, but with overlap between the types. This model assumes that most people's behavior toward children is guided by limits. Thus most parents who use physical punishment will not inflict serious injury on their children (although some injuries do occur as a result of loss of control, poor aim, or random unexpected factors). Their behavior is unlikely to lead to serious or life-threatening injury. But there are some parents who, for whatever social and psychological reasons, do set out to injure, maim, torture, or kill their children. Sometimes their attempts fail and the children are not injured or killed, but the upper threshold for these parents' behavior is so high that injury and death are much more likely outcomes of their behavior than they would be for other types of parents.

The assumption that child abuse is not a continuum but rather that distinct types of violent behavior exist requires that theorists inject a note of caution into their formulations. Thus homicide is not simply an "extreme form of interpersonal vio-

Figure 3.3
Two Distinct Types of Abusers, with Overlap

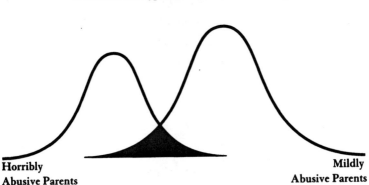

Horribly Abusive Parents

Mildly Abusive Parents

lence." Rather, homicide is a distinct form of behavior that requires a distinct explanation. Such an explanation, while valuable for understanding homicide, is not directly generalizable to other, less severe forms of family violence. Nor are models of less severe forms of abuse automatically applicable to child homicide.

PARENTS' WILLINGNESS TO CHANGE

A major failing in child abuse assessments is the crude way behavior change is conceptualized and measured. First, behavior change is conceived as a one-step process: The abuser simply changes from one form of behavior to another. For example, for an alcoholic or drug abuser, change involves stopping using alcohol or drugs. Someone who stops, but then begins again, has failed to change. Second, caseworkers often use compliance with case plans as an indicator of change. Thus parents who attend parenting classes or go to counseling are seen as changing—even if these same parents continue to deny abuse and neglect. Complying with a court-ordered program of services or classes is not the same as actually changing.

Social scientists who study behavior change across a wide range of behavior now realize that change is not simply a one-step process, that relapse is part of the overall change process, and that measuring change and likelihood of change is much more complex than the simple item on the assessment form that assesses "Caretaker's level of cooperation."

The psychologists James Prochaska and Carlo DiClemente

have developed "The Transtheoretical Model of Change," which posits a dynamic process involving progression through five stages:[24]

Precontemplation. The individual either does not think he or she has a problem that needs changing, or does not wish to change.

Contemplation. Recognition of a problem that needs changing and preliminary thinking about what to do about it.

Preparation. A finer discrimination of the contemplation stage that moves beyond idle thinking and involves preparing for action.

Action. The individual has begun to act on the problem and to make changes in the behavior.

Maintenance. The behavior has changed, but the individual still must actively work to maintain the changes.

Relapse. For most people relapse is not a stage, but is a part of the change process and is recognized as such. In fact, the stages of change are viewed as cyclical in that one may relapse from action or maintenance to an earlier stage, but then may cycle back up, perhaps more quickly than the first time around.

Termination. Termination occurs when there is no temptation to engage in the negative behavior and no risk of relapse. The problem is no longer an issue.

Data from a variety of studies indicate that the amount of progress people make in changing their behavior following intervention is directly related to the stage they were in prior to intervention. The further along people are in the stages of change prior to intervention, the more they progress afterward. The stages are also powerful predictors of who drops out of treatment programs.

"We invest countless hours and incredible time, energy, and services in the families we serve, and they don't seem to change." This is the complaint of a former director of a Department of Children and Their Families. Interventions can work only if they are matched to a client's stage of change. Thus we need to develop techniques of risk assessment that measure a caretaker's or family's stage of change and then match interventions to the stages. This would minimize the continuing problem of providing massive resources for a family that is unable or unwilling to change its behavior.

CREATING A SAFE WORLD

Reporting was not the weak link that prevented the Department of Children and Their Families from saving David Edwards's life. David and his family, like 3 million other families that year, had been reported for suspected child abuse. David was born while his family was an open child abuse and neglect case. The department received two additional reports of suspected maltreatment: anonymous reports from a neighbor.

One reason David Edwards died is that the DCF workers were untrained and unskilled in the process of risk assessment. The risk assessment form is, at best, an impressionistic, unscientific instrument that includes assessments of real risk factors as well as factors that are supported only by conventional wisdom, not scientific evidence. The most significant risk factor, the previous severe abuse of Marie, was minimized. The cleanliness of the apartment was overemphasized. Donald and Darlene's resistance to change was categorized as anger, not as a significant risk factor.

The most important step that *must* be taken by the child welfare system and researchers alike is to develop a comprehensive, sound, and valid assessment of risk that measures both risk factors for maltreatment *and* stage of change of caretakers and families suspected of child maltreatment.

4

Unreasonable Efforts

IF WE LOOK AT THE CASE OF DAVID EDWARDS IN THE SAME way investigator Justine Peters did—ignoring his sister's life-threatening head injury—then it would be difficult to definitively determine his risk of future abuse. He had no telltale handprints or easily identifiable inflicted injuries. His weight fluctuated, so it was hard to pinpoint whether he was a failure-to-thrive baby or not. Darlene's depression was a risk factor, but a subtle one. David's case was both difficult and typical.

The case of Marie Edwards, however, was much less complex. At the age of six weeks, she had received a near-fatal injury that all the signs indicated one or both of her parents had caused. The level of harm to Marie was so great and the level of risk she faced so substantial, especially given her age, that she could not, and did not, remain in the home with her parents. She spent eighteen months in foster care, not because the state couldn't find a suitable permanent placement for her—her foster parents had decided they wanted to adopt her within weeks of her placement—but because for fifteen of the eighteen months, the Department of Children and Their Families was working to *reunite* Marie with the parents who had nearly killed her. Why would a state agency leave a child in limbo and work to put her back in harm's way?

The reason was the guiding policy of child welfare agencies, the policy of "reasonable efforts," which is thought to be "in the best interests of children" but often compromises their safety.

THE ORIGIN OF "REASONABLE EFFORTS"

In the 1960s through the 1970s, child welfare policy had focused on removing children from dangerous homes. As the number of reports of abuse swelled, so did the number of children removed from their parents. By the late 1970s nearly 1 million reports of child abuse and neglect were made each year, and an estimated 500,000 children were in foster care.[1]

In time, horror stories of children wrongly removed from their homes began to spread through the child welfare community, were picked up by the media, and child protection agencies began to be viewed as "child snatchers"—too quick on the trigger to remove children from their homes. These concerns were amplified by the fact that children often languished in foster care or, in some cases, residential care for months and years while child protection agencies made stumbling efforts to move the case along in the legal system. The average length of stay in foster care in the late 1970s appeared to be nearly two and a half years.[2] More and more children were being "lost" to "foster care drift." Too many children were going into foster care, too few were coming out. Furthermore, the costs appeared to be rising geometrically.

Children are killed and injured by foster parents as well as by biological parents. In Rhode Island in the mid-1970s, a youngster named Keith Chisholm was removed from his mother by the Department of Social and Rehabilitative Services.[3] Keith had not been physically or sexually abused; rather, he was a victim of neglect. The boy was later beaten to death by his foster father, a man who had previously been arrested for assault and battery. Cases like these made child protection workers in Rhode Island very reluctant to take any but the most grievously injured children away from their birth parents.

A new child protection policy emerged in the late 1970s and was crystallized by the federal Adoption Assistance and Child Welfare Act of 1980, which experts and advocates generally consider the most significant legislation in the history of child welfare. Two overriding philosophies emerged from the act. The first was *permanency planning*, which assumed that prompt and decisive action to maintain children safely in their homes, or to place them as quickly as possible in permanent homes with other families, was the most desirable goal of child welfare services. The second philosophy was embodied in the words *reasonable efforts:*

> in each case, reasonable efforts will be made (A) prior to the placement of a child in foster care, to prevent or eliminate the need for removal of the child from his home, and (B) to make it possible for the child to return to his home.[4]

States had to demonstrate that they made reasonable efforts and that they were in compliance with the permanency planning provision of the law in order to qualify for federal funding for adoption and foster care.

Despite the law's good intentions, it planted seeds of trouble. The goal of child protection services became safeguarding children while also working to reunite them with their abusive parents. The assumption was that these mandates could be balanced successfully. The reality was that the demands were contradictory.

One problem was the ambiguity around the very concept of "reasonable efforts." Nowhere in the federal legislation, state policy, or ensuing legal decisions in state courts were "reasonable efforts" ever clearly defined. As a result, child protection workers, administrators, and legal staff had no guidelines for how much or how long they had to make "efforts" at reunification before moving to permanent placements for abused and neglected children. Similarly, the inherent and dangerous contradiction between ensuring safety and attempting to reunite abusive parents with abused children was never publicly acknowledged by federal or state officials.

"Reasonable Efforts" in Action

By June 1988, when assessment worker Lisa Hanratty took over Marie Edwards's case, the principles of the 1980 act were firmly in place. Hanratty knew she had to first protect Marie from further harm, then work to reunite her with her parents. Marie's injuries—head injury and broken bones—were so serious that there was no question about what Hanratty's first priority must be: find a short-term placement for Marie while the department made "reasonable efforts" to improve Donald and Darlene Edwards's parenting skills so that Marie could rejoin them. The injuries were so serious that they overrode any need to use the department risk assessment form—Marie would be placed as soon as she was released from the hospital.

Kinship Placement

The first goal in placement is to try to find a relative who will take the child in. This, of course, is a rather odd approach, given the substantial amount of research evidence that indicates patterns of abuse and neglect are often (but not always) passed along from generation to generation (even though we know that not every abused child grows up to be abusive, and not every abusive adult was abused as a child).[5]

Investigator Albert Huey had noted in his report that Darlene's mother and stepfather, who had baby-sat Marie on occasion, had indicated some interest in taking her home with them from the hospital. Of course, no one had given any consideration to the possibility of an intergenerational transmission of abuse. Little risk assessment was done on the maternal grandparents' child-rearing skills, abilities, or potentials. As it turned out, none of this would have mattered. Darlene's mother and stepfather told Hanratty when she visited them on June 8, 1988, that they were no longer willing to take physical custody of Marie. Although they did not say so directly, Hanratty got the impression that they had somehow been intimidated by Donald Edwards into retracting their offer.

Hanratty also detected some concern on the part of Darlene's mother about how Darlene "handled" Marie. Although there was no direct accusation, Hanratty certainly got the very strong impression that Darlene's mother believed Darlene was the one who had battered little Marie.

The Foster Care Placement

By June 13, Marie's condition had stabilized to the point where she was ready to be discharged from the hospital. Her legs were in casts. The subdural hematoma had subsided, but Marie had suffered some brain damage and was prone to seizures. She would require daily medication to control the seizures for the foreseeable future, and possibly for the rest of her life. Although out of medical danger, Marie was far from normal. Lisa Hanratty noted in her file that Marie was "very fragile and stiff . . . she is not very responsive."

Having failed to find an appropriate family placement, Hanratty recommended a foster-family placement and Marie was discharged into the care of June and Dennis Ganley, a registered nurse and a high-school guidance counselor in their early thirties who had been foster parents for six years and had two school-age children of their own. They had cared for special-needs children like Marie previously.

With Marie in the Ganley home, Lisa Hanratty turned her attention to her second task, assessing Marie's parents and making a reunification plan. Hanratty scheduled an appointment with Darlene for mid-afternoon on June 14. Darlene was home alone—Donald was at his job at the jewelry manufacturer.

Although Darlene was still a bit depressed, her spirits seemed slightly brighter. She told Hanratty, "Now that the baby is out of the picture, I can do pretty much what I want to do." This was hardly the testimony of a mother eager to get her baby back. But the policy of reunification dictated Hanratty's course of action; she made plans to refer Donald and Darlene to a local mental health agency for an assessment and counseling toward reunification with Marie.

The Psychologist Visit

Two weeks after Hanratty's home visit, Darlene and Donald Edwards had their first contact with Marie since she was hospitalized. The visit was not merely a chance for the parents to see and hold their daughter, it was the first stage of a "psychosocial" evaluation of them and the first stage of the department's reunification plan. The visit took place at the Queen City Mental Health Center, in a city miles from where Donald and Darlene lived. The inconveniently located clinic was chosen because it was *the* contracted mental health clinic in the state where psychosocial evaluations were conducted.

Darlene and Donald arrived first, around 2:00 P.M. Lisa Hanratty arrived fifteen minutes later with Marie. Part of the reason Hanratty was late was the somewhat heated discussion she had had with Marie's foster mother, who was appalled that the department was giving any consideration to sending Marie back to her biological parents. Although June Ganley knew that by speaking up she was risking having Marie removed from her house, she vigorously confronted Hanratty, arguing that Marie had not even begun to recover from her nearly fatal injuries and already the department was trying to give her back to the parents who had inflicted them.

All four sat in the waiting room for twenty minutes until the psychologist was ready for them. The wait was intentional; it gave Hanratty—who would not be in the room during the psychologist's evaluation—a chance to observe how Donald and Darlene interacted with Marie.

Hanratty was taken aback by both parents' lack of interest in their baby. Neither asked or offered to hold little Marie and neither would hold her until told to do so by Hanratty. When Helen Benedick, the psychologist assigned to the Edwards family, came out of her office, introduced herself to Donald and Darlene, and suggested that Darlene carry Marie into the office, Darlene lifted Marie under the armpits and marched her into the office with the child facing away from her. At no time during the fifty-minute meeting did Donald make any attempt to touch or hold Marie, and Darlene held her only when Helen Benedick instructed her to do so.

Donald's anger became palpable over the course of the fifty minutes. It was directed at everyone. He would not cooperate with Benedick, would not interact with Marie, and glared contemptuously at his wife during most of the session. At one point he blurted out, "We'll get even someday. Maybe that worker will have her kid killed in a car accident or get run over by a drunk driver. I'm going to have my payback." It was clear to Donald that he had lost Marie. "Who's going to give back a kid who had a cracked skull and cracked legs? No one, never. I don't know how this happened. I can't explain. But it don't matter. The kid ain't comin' back to us."

Neither Benedick nor Hanratty was encouraged by this first session. Benedick wrote in her clinical notes that, based on the observations she made at the session, Marie should not be returned home at this time. She specifically cited the intensity of Donald's rejection of his wife and Marie, and Darlene's complete inability to show warmth and empathy toward her baby. Benedick ended by stating she had deep concerns about the parents' ability to meet this child's basic needs and to avoid doing her further harm.

Nearly six months would go by before Benedick saw Darlene, Donald, and Marie Edwards again. This fifty-minute session constituted the entire professional evaluation and counseling the Edwards family would get during that six-month period.

A Supervised Home Visit

Three days after the psychosocial evaluation, Lisa Hanratty moved ahead with the second step in her reunification plan: a supervised home visit for Marie with Donald and Darlene. Again, Hanratty had to drive to the foster home and pick up Marie and then drive twenty minutes to the Edwardses' apartment. Assessment and Direct Services workers are responsible for transporting children to and from hospital, office, and home visits. The travel and observation time involved means a single visit can consume half a workday.

Hanratty arrived at the Edwardses' at 4:30 P.M. She wanted a chance to observe both Donald and Darlene, and Donald insisted that the visit be late in the day so that he would not have to miss work for the second time that week.

Darlene was less tense and less cold with Marie this time, but she was hardly warm either. Perhaps the familiar surroundings helped, or perhaps she felt that she was being watched a bit less in her own home. Donald, however, was even angrier at home than he was in Benedick's office, pacing around the apartment for the full hour of the visit, alternately mumbling under his breath and blurting out some diatribe against the department. Neither Donald nor Darlene picked up, touched, or even interacted with Marie. Hanratty was relieved when the visit ended and she could return Marie to her foster home.

A Possible Change of Custody

On July 1 the Department of Children and Their Families asked the Family Court to continue legal custody with the state and to transfer physical custody of Marie Edwards to her maternal grandparents, who had changed their minds since their meeting with Lisa Hanratty on June 8 and were now interested in having Marie in their home. No consideration was given to how Marie was doing with her foster parents because the 1980 Adoption Assistance and Child Welfare Act requires child welfare agencies to find children the "least restrictive" placement, and "kinship care" is considered less restrictive (and is less costly) than foster care.

In petitioning the Family Court, the department presented the preliminary assessment prepared by Lisa Hanratty, which included observations of the psychosocial evaluation of June 27 and the home visit of June 30. The court approved the continuation of legal custody with the state and granted the motion to change physical custody to the maternal grandparents.

Eleven days later, Marie's grandparents changed their minds again. Hanratty was unable to find out why. All Darlene's mother would say was that she and her husband were concerned about Donald and Darlene's "attitude" toward them. Hanratty was convinced that Donald had blown up at Darlene's parents when he heard they would get custody of Marie. At any rate, Marie would be staying with her foster family for the time being.

The Direct Services Worker

On July 18, Lisa Hanratty was removed from the Marie Edwards case: the six-week maximum the department allowed for assessment had been reached. Hanratty would have no further contact with Donald, Darlene, or Marie Edwards. She would never be asked for advice or consulted by anyone who subsequently worked with either Marie or David Edwards.

Marie's case was transferred to a Direct Services worker, Karen Hastings, who had recently transferred into Direct Services from the state Department of Mental Health. She had a bachelor's degree in human services but had taken no courses in social work, family violence, or child abuse. Nor had she ever attended any in-service training on child abuse. The experience Hastings brought to the case was her work in the Department of Mental Health and the twenty hours of departmental training. At the time she was assigned Marie's case, she had a caseload of twenty-seven children and their families.

Hastings had been briefed by her supervisor on her mandate and responsibilities. She was to work toward reuniting Marie with Donald and Darlene by arranging supervised visits and trying to identify appropriate services for the parents. This last task would be made much more difficult because

Hastings never read Lisa Hanratty's assessment report. Had she done so, Hastings would have learned that

> Darlene is a young mother, isolated for long hours and has no friends. She describes her life as totally changed after the arrival of the baby. She has reported feelings of detachment and being unhappy as the primary caretaker of the child. [She] asks about "postpartum depression." In my opinion, mother may have caused the injuries to her infant. Although the evidence is circumstantial, it does point to mother. Mother should have a psychiatric evaluation. There should be family counseling for mother and father. There should be medical follow-up for Marie, and weekly supervised visitation and parenting classes.

The only part of this brief plan recommended by Hanratty that was initially implemented were the weekly and then bi-weekly supervised and then unsupervised visits scheduled over the next year.

On the day the case was assigned to Karen Hastings, she received an angry call from Donald Edwards complaining that a supervised visit between Donald, Darlene, and Marie had not yet been scheduled.

Hastings was finally able to schedule the first of the weekly supervised family visits for July 22. (These would become unsupervised visits in March 1989.) The one- or two-hour visits took place weekly at first and then were increased to twice a week over the next twelve months—up until the birth of David Edwards.

Both June and Dennis Ganley remained skeptical of the

reunification plan. They were growing more attached to Marie with each week and more terrified that the department would actually return her to her biological parents. They were powerless, however, to do anything or say much. They knew that if foster parents persisted in questioning the department plan, the department would simply move the child to another foster home.

The visits went well, Hastings would later recall. Darlene continued to be distant from her daughter but Donald did interact with her. Hastings decided to suggest counseling for Darlene for depression. It was the only specific mental health service that was ever recommended, but it was never provided over the next twelve months that the Edwards family was an open case and the department was making "reasonable efforts" to reunite the family. Two and a half years later, during hearings conducted to review David Edwards's death, Hastings was asked why no counseling for depression was ever provided for Darlene. She explained: "[Darlene] wanted a female counselor, and the department could not find a female counselor who was available"—that is, who was on the department's "approved provider" list. In the end, "reasonable efforts" included no psychological assistance for Darlene Edwards, even when she became pregnant with her second child and postpartum depression had been suspected after her first child was born.

As for Donald, he flatly refused to consider counseling. Nor did any marital counseling take place. The only formal "service" that was rendered was the continuation of the psychosocial family assessment begun at the end of June by Helen Benedick.

From July to December, the involvement between the Department of Children and Their Families and the Edwardses was limited to the supervised home visits and occasional meetings with Helen Benedick at the mental health center. During these months the case was a low-priority one for both Karen Hastings and the department. Marie was out of the home and at no risk of being reinjured by her parents.

In August 1988, at age four months, Marie Edwards was referred to a neurosurgeon and to the George Street School for Special Needs for an evaluation. Damage to both sides of her brain was found; the school recommended that she be enrolled when she was old enough. In September, Family Court continued physical and legal custody of Marie with the department. Neither Donald nor Darlene appeared in court for the ten-minute hearing. Helen Benedick's report, based on the June 27 meeting and her review of the available case materials, was sent to Karen Hastings in the second week of October. The report concluded with the statement, "I cannot recommend this child's return to her natural family at this time."

The Plea Bargain

The Edwardses' attorney and the Department of Children and Their Families reached a plea-bargain agreement. In return for the department's withdrawing the charge of child abuse, Donald and Darlene would plead guilty to child neglect. Marie would be committed to the care, custody, and control of the department director. On December 7 Donald and Darlene were directed by the court to attend family counseling at the same mental health center where they had been seen by Helen Benedick. Karen Hastings would develop a case plan for the family that included marital counseling. This plan did not include psychiatric evaluations or individual counseling for either Darlene or Donald. It did not include any ameliorative social or economic resources for the family. No plan was provided to deal with Darlene's symptoms of depression. In short, the plea bargain stabilized the physical and legal custody of Marie and ended the department's attempts to prove that Marie's injuries had been inflicted by one or both of her parents.

Family Counseling

On January 3, 1989, Donald, Darlene, and Marie (who had been taken there from her foster home by Karen Hastings) met with Helen Benedick at the Queen City Mental Health Center for their first family counseling session.

The Edwardses were somewhat more relaxed during the January session compared to their behavior at the evaluation session six months earlier. They interacted with Marie and each other, and the palpable air of hostility, especially from Donald, was absent.

Marie was noticeably developmentally delayed in her speech and her movement. She did not crawl and made few vocal noises. Her posture was rigid. When Helen Benedick discussed Marie's condition with the parents, Darlene said that she thought Marie probably had cerebral palsy. Perhaps, Darlene noted, the cerebral palsy was the cause of the fractured ribs and legs. At no point did Darlene or Donald acknowledge any involvement in the physical abuse of Marie; they apparently had decided to deny that any physical abuse had occurred at all.

Both Darlene and Donald still held Marie facing away from them. They made little direct eye contact with their daughter and showed almost no nurturing behavior. Darlene made numerous critical comments about how Marie looked and how she behaved. At one point Darlene teased Marie by keeping her bottle just out of her reach. Even when Marie cried and wailed in frustration, Darlene did not give her the bottle and Donald made no attempt to intervene.

Nearly three weeks elapsed between the first family counseling session and the next one (in general, the counseling sessions were scheduled monthly). During that period, Karen Hastings had made a scheduled home visit, on January 4. It had not gone well. Donald raged at Hastings that DCF was out to get him. He became even more upset when she suggested he and Darlene voluntarily terminate their parental rights. "There is no way," Donald screamed, "that you will get this baby or the next." This was the first suggestion that Darlene might be pregnant again.

On January 11 Hastings had made another scheduled visit to the Edwards apartment. This time she brought the case plan she had drafted, which included the provision that Donald and Darlene continue to participate in family counseling and that they both take parenting classes. Besides these "soft" services, the case plan provided for housekeeping help in the event that Marie returned home. The housekeeper was provided not because Darlene needed help with the housework; her house was always neat and well-organized. The housekeeper's main function was to be in the home so that Darlene could go out if she wanted. More important than being a baby-sitter, the housekeeper would be able to monitor Darlene's behavior. The housekeeper as a resource and monitor would, it was hoped, reduce the chances of Darlene loosing her temper and abusing her child.

Donald refused to sign the case plan. He was specifically opposed to the demand that he attend the parenting classes. He said he would go to the classes, but he wouldn't sign the plan because he believed that if he signed and then failed to attend the classes, the department would go to court to terminate his parental rights.

The January 26 counseling session/parenting class was an outright disaster. Benedick began the meeting by explaining some of her basic goals for the session to Donald and Darlene. Suddenly, in the middle of Benedick's talk, Darlene stood up and stomped out of the room. Donald jumped up and followed his wife out. Benedick was left in the room with Marie, who was sitting in the middle of the floor playing with blocks. Benedick could not follow Donald and Darlene out and leave Marie alone, and the couple did not return. Finally, after a ten-minute wait that seemed like an hour, Benedick gathered up Marie and went to look for Donald and Darlene. Benedick found them just outside the women's restroom. As she approached Donald, he insisted, in a voice just under a yell, that he wanted his daughter back—a term he meant figuratively, since he made no move at all to take Marie from Benedick's arms and hold her.

Suddenly Darlene interrupted. "I'm pregnant," she blurted out. "I'm not sure I want this child [Marie]. There's nothing between us. I don't feel anything toward her."

Ignoring his wife's announcement, Donald then said: "I want the foster placement changed. This kid doesn't even know us. She doesn't recognize us as her parents. She thinks her foster parents are her real parents. That isn't right. I want the placement changed or I'm going to do something to those foster parents. Something's going to happen to them, I can tell you."

Finally, Donald acknowledged Darlene's statement about her pregnancy by saying: "You have that kid, but you're not going to get this kid from us." And with that, Donald and Darlene walked out of the Queen City Mental Health Center and left Helen Benedick, mouth agape, holding Marie Edwards. The counseling sessions nevertheless continued on roughly a monthly basis until July.

Evidence to Terminate?

Given the events of January 26, a naive observer would assume that, nearly ten months after the Department of Children and Their Families became involved with the Edwards family, it would have enough evidence to terminate Donald and Darlene's parental rights and make a permanent plan for Marie's care and upbringing. More important, a naive observer might assume that red flags shot up like fireworks when Darlene announced she was pregnant. Neither happened.

The "reasonable efforts" doctrine gave both Helen Benedick

and Karen Hastings tunnel vision. Both knew they were obliged to make reasonable efforts, and both knew those reasonable efforts had to continue until they yielded convincing evidence that they would not work. Of course, neither knew what that convincing evidence was, so they both continued to provide supervised visitation and counseling and parenting sessions, even in the face of the fact that neither Donald nor Darlene showed any change and that with each month, they were more and more detached from the life of their daughter—with whom they had spent only the first six weeks of her life.

The pregnancy did not raise red flags because prevailing policy was to view each child in the family independently. No one assumed, in spite of a great deal of evidence from scientific research, that just because someone abused one child he or she would abuse another. For all intents and purposes, the pregnancy was, and would continue to be, ignored.

One supervised home visit produced a warning sign that was noticed but had no impact on changing the course of the department's "reasonable efforts" and would ultimately never be considered when the department was asked to assess the risk to David Edwards. Darlene was home alone during this visit— Donald was working an extra shift at the jewelry plant. Marie was cranky when she arrived for the visit and became even more so during the often forced and uncertain interaction with her mother. Darlene became increasingly frustrated with Marie as the visit went on, and finally, when Marie began to cry and wail, Darlene turned to Karen Hastings and said, "You take her—try to get this kid to shut up for me." Hastings, taken aback by Darlene's intolerance and impatience, asked her how she planned to manage if she had two crying babies in the home.

"I don't know how the hell I'm going to do it, I really don't. I'm not sure I want this kid back. . . ." Darlene hesitated and went silent.

In spite of this incident, Hastings moved to unsupervised weekly visits in March, which continued until June 28, just before David's birth. These visits, usually lasting a few hours, were essentially unremarkable. On April 11 Donald and Darlene had an unsupervised overnight visit with Marie. The visit was uneventful, but it *was* remarkable, because, according to Karen Hastings's clinical notes, at no time on April 11 or 12 when she came to pick up Marie did she hear Donald or Darlene mention that the day before—April 10—was Marie's first birthday. Hastings saw no evidence of a birthday celebration: no cake, no decorations, no presents, no balloons. Was it possible, Hastings wondered, that neither Donald nor Darlene had remembered Marie's birthday? Hastings concluded her notes that "bonding between parents and child is still questionable."

The inherent inconsistency between the policy of "reasonable efforts" and the mandate to protect vulnerable children came into sharp relief as the case continued. The Edwardses were given continued family counseling, and their access to Marie was expanded. However, no date was set for making a decision to reunite the family or to terminate parental rights.

A Court Review

The Family Court reviewed the Edwards case June 7—nine months after the last case review. The Department of Children and Their Families, in the person of Karen Hastings and a lawyer from its legal staff, recommended that physical and legal custody remain with the department—that Marie stay with her foster parents and that the department maintain legal custody.

Donald and Darlene were divided on custody. Donald urged his attorney to demand that Marie be returned home. Darlene, however, was reluctant to have Marie come home. Given that her baby was due to be born in four weeks, Darlene thought it would be better to delay reunification. The judge agreed with Darlene and the department, and continued Marie's custody with the department and scheduled another hearing for the first week of September.

As a means of expanding the department's efforts at family reunification, Karen Hastings modified her case plan and included the first "hard" service for the Edwardses. A parent aide would be assigned to assist Darlene in the home. The parent aide would be expected to come to the house at least five days a week and help Darlene prepare for the birth of her new baby and also prepare for Marie's return home. But, like the housekeeper mentioned earlier, the parent aide would also be a resource and monitor—watchful for abuse and neglect and present so as to deter any anger or frustration from turning into abuse and neglect. However, given the events of the next six weeks, the parent aide would never actually visit the Edwards apartment.

Creating a Safe World

We must escape from the trap of the "one size fits all" theories and interventions based on an exclusive belief in social and environmental causes of abuse. We need to abandon the notion that one intervention or treatment can help "cure" all abusers, and recognize that in the most serious cases of abuse, the parents are probably constitutionally different from those who do not seriously abuse or kill their children.

Reasonable efforts become unreasonable when they are applied to individuals or families for whom the services cannot work or who are simply not amenable to changing their dangerous and harmful behaviors.

5

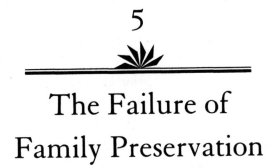

The Failure of
Family Preservation

David Edwards was born July 5, 1989, at Providence Hospital. Darlene and her baby went home three days later. On July 21, everything came to a head at a regularly scheduled family counseling/parenting class session. The session began with Marie sitting on the floor, playing with toys, Darlene feeding David, and Donald sitting off to the side of the room. Benedick began with small talk about newborn David and how he was doing. Halfway through the fifty-minute session, Darlene got up and said, "OK to use the bathroom?" and left the room, taking David with her. Fifteen minutes later Benedick's secretary opened the door and said, "I thought you might want to know that Mrs. Edwards has left the building." Benedick was nonplussed, but she simply continued the session with Donald and Marie. Donald continued to interact and play with Marie and seemed unmoved by the departure of his wife and newborn son.

When the session was over, Benedick walked out with Donald and Marie. They found Darlene sitting in the Edwardses' car in the parking lot. David was asleep in his car seat.

"It took you long enough!" Darlene screamed. She got out of the car. "I'm never coming back here. I've made up my mind. I'm giving her up for adoption. He [Donald] acts all sweet and everything, but he doesn't help. I don't want to deprive her, but I know he would."

Donald was furious. He threw open the rear door of the car, slung Marie into the second car seat, and roughly strapped her in. Benedick became concerned about Marie's safety. She suggested to Donald and Darlene—but mostly to Donald— that they leave Marie with her and that she would call Karen Hastings and have Marie returned to her foster family. "Maybe," Benedick said as calmly as she could, "this isn't the best time for a visit." By this time Donald had started the car and had begun to drive slowly away. Without even waiting for Donald to stop the car, Darlene swung her door open, jumped out, and flung the front seat of the two-door car forward. She reached across the sleeping David and unbuckled Marie. Darlene nearly threw Marie at Benedick and, without a word, jumped back into the front seat and slammed the door. As Benedick stood holding Marie in the hot July sun, in the middle of the parking lot, Donald accelerated and flew out of the parking lot.

Hastings consulted with Benedick to get a full accounting of the events of July 21, then met with Dan O'Brien of the legal staff to review the department's legal options. Finally, she reviewed the case with her supervisor. All parties agreed that they could now cease their "reasonable efforts" toward family reunification. If they could get the Edwardses to formalize Darlene's intention to voluntarily terminate her parental rights, they could close the case and find a permanent placement for Marie. David Edwards was never mentioned in any of the discussions.

The various meetings and reports were completed by the first week of August. Karen Hastings scheduled a visit at the Edwards apartment. Darlene Edwards was still insistent that she did not want Marie back. Donald, angry and frustrated, tried to argue that he wanted Marie, but eventually gave some ground and asked whether it would be possible to have her placed with one of his relatives. Hastings, for the first time, revealed that Marie's foster parents were interested in adopting her. The Ganleys had continued to confront Hastings with their concerns about Marie's safety and pressured Hastings to try to make it possible for them to adopt her. Donald finally gave in and agreed to voluntarily terminate his parental rights. Hastings never once asked to see or examine David Edwards, who slept in his crib in the other room during the visit.

The regularly scheduled Family Court hearing was held September 7. Dan O'Brien and Karen Hastings, in consultation with the Edwardses' lawyer, informed the judge that the Edwardses were willing to voluntarily terminate their parental rights to Marie. In return for this agreement, the Edwardses' lawyer wanted the Department of Children and Their Families to drop any further legal action regarding the abuse of Marie and to have the file indicate that there was no evidence Marie was abused by either Donald or Darlene. O'Brien agreed to the plea bargain, and the court hearing was over in five minutes. The agreement, while it did not actually expunge the file, meant that the department could not use the abuse of Marie as a reason to intervene on behalf of David without a substantiated charge of abuse of David. On September 27, Dan O'Brien, Donald and Darlene Edwards, and their attorney went to Family Court to sign the final order voluntarily terminating the Edwardses' parental rights to Marie. The case was closed. A year later, David was dead.

GOOD INTENTIONS: DID THEY WORK?

When the panel that investigated the death of David Edwards interviewed them, Karen Hastings, Helen Benedick, and the top administrators of the Department of Children and Their Families argued that they had successfully balanced the mandate for family reunification with the mandate to protect a vulnerable child in Marie's case. When the efforts to reunite the family did not work out, Marie's safety was assured by her remaining with, and ultimately being adopted by, her foster parents.

Of course, the only way one could conceivably argue that the system worked in Marie's case is to ignore the fact that Darlene Edwards killed Marie's brother one year after the case was closed by the department. But even if David had never been born, or even if he had not been killed by his mother, the case of Marie Edwards is not one that can be cited to support the policy of family reunification.

The outcome of the case was more a product of dumb luck than good casework or sound case management. Even at the moment when Darlene Edwards terminated her own parental rights in the parking lot of the Queen City Mental Health Center, Hastings, Benedick, and the department were continuing to work toward the goal of family reunification. Had Darlene not thrust Marie into Helen Benedick's arms, Benedick and Hastings were prepared to let Marie go home with Darlene and Donald for an unsupervised overnight visit.

This case was like the majority of cases of family reunification efforts. In a manner of speaking, the Department of Children and Their Families played Russian roulette with Marie: expanding supervised and unsupervised visits while looking for concrete evidence, such as another injury, that the Edwardses were unfit parents.

The case plan of counseling and parenting classes; scheduled and unscheduled visits to the home by Karen Hastings; a parent aide for Darlene; and expanded unsupervised visits for Marie with the parents who had nearly killed her was followed, *in spite of* mounting evidence that Donald and Darlene never were and were not becoming caring, nurturing, concerned, or even barely adequate parents. For all intents and purposes, the only consequence of Karen Hastings's and Helen Benedick's subsequent involvement with the family was that it apparently wore down Darlene Edwards and motivated her to terminate her parental rights. No one involved in the case set a deadline for ending the reunification efforts. No one took stock of the family and made a determination about whether the efforts were likely to succeed.

The claim that the system worked in this case also ignores the emotional toll it took on Marie's foster parents, the Ganleys. They were prepared to adopt her within a month of beginning to care for her. They waited in anguish for more than a year while the department pursued its reunification plan. In the end, their patience was rewarded and they were able to adopt Marie. But for a year of their lives, and the first year of Marie's life, the Ganleys held back from becoming too attached to her, fearing they could lose her any day. Any student of child development would agree that Marie would have been far better off in a permanent placement for the first year of her life than in a tenuous and stressful temporary foster placement.

If family reunification worked as a public policy, the Edwards case would not have been closed when Donald and Darlene terminated their parental rights to Marie. Karen Hastings, Helen Benedick, the legal staff involved in the case, and the department administrators would have recognized the major risk to the new baby and would have monitored the family closely. They might have also considered removing David Edwards from harm's way on the July afternoon when Darlene figuratively terminated her parental rights to Marie. They did neither.

Intensive Family Preservation Services: The Homebuilders Model

An alternative to my pessimistic and critical analysis of how the Department of Children and Their Families managed the case of Marie Edwards would argue that the reunification efforts did not work because they were the wrong kind of efforts. In the traditional, open-ended family reunification programs administered by the child welfare bureaucracy, "soft" services, such as therapy and education, are provided in the offices of child welfare workers or agencies subcontracted to provide them, during the normal 9-to-5 workday, in the standard fifty-minute clinical hour. Clients typically must arrange for transportation to and from the office in order to receive the services. Caseloads average fifteen to fifty families per worker, and waiting in the office is a routine part of the process. Because needs exceed available workers and services, there are often waiting lists for all services. Worker burnout tends to be high due to the frustration of large caseloads and limited resources.

Clients often cannot, or will not, meet their scheduled appointments. Clinicians, overwhelmed with active cases, merely label the file of the unkept appointment a "DINK" (Did Not Keep) and move to the next case. Few clinicians take the time to bring the clients who failed to keep appointments to court to terminate their parental rights, so there is no sure penalty for not partaking of services. This form of "reasonable efforts" often means offering services, but not necessarily delivering them.

An alternative to the "business as usual" efforts at family reunification is family preservation.[1] The family preservation revolution began in Tacoma, Washington, in 1974—six years before the enactment of the Adoption Assistance and Child Welfare Act. David Haapala and Jill Kinney, a married couple who were child psychologists, submitted with a group of social workers a grant application to the National Institute of Mental Health (NIMH) for funding for a "super foster home." The proposal called for a facility that would help foster parents in Tacoma cope with "out of control" adolescents. Jack Bartleson, the contact person at NIMH, suggested a counterproposal: Why not work with families *before* a child is removed? Instead of putting resources into foster care, why not devote them to trying to keep the original birth family together? More important, Bartleson suggested, why not provide the services in the home—have the social workers actually move in with the family?[2]

Of course, few social workers would be willing to move in with abusive families. Some warned that those who did would need "bulletproof sleeping bags."[3] Not surprisingly, Haapala, Kinney, and the social workers in their group decided they would not have to. According to Kinney, "We found out right away that you didn't need to actually move in. . . . If you did a good job listening, people would calm down. Things would begin to look clearer, and emotions would subside."[4]

Haapala and Kinney's program, which they named Homebuilders, became the model of intensive family preservation services. The goal of Homebuilders and all family preservation programs is to maintain children safely in their homes or to facilitate a safe and lasting reunification. Homebuilders services are supposed to be limited to families that have a serious crisis threatening their stability and the safety of family members, or where reunification is being pursued after an abused child has been placed outside the home.

The essential feature of family preservation is that it is an intensive, short-term, crisis intervention. Services are provided in the client's home. The length of session is variable— it is not confined to the fifty-minute clinical hour. Services are available daily, seven days a week, twenty-four hours a day, not just during business hours Monday through Friday. Caseloads are small—two or three families per worker. Both soft and hard services are provided. Unlike traditional family reunification services, Homebuilders has a predetermined *length and cost;* typically, the length of services is four to six weeks. Limiting the length of services means that more clients can be served, and that the cost per family can be predetermined, budgeted, and managed. It is this last feature, cost containment, that ultimately proved to be the most salable feature of the Homebuilders model of family preservation.

The newest and fastest-growing school of thought in child welfare is that intensive family preservation services such as Homebuilders do work. They work because they resolve the exact problems that limited Karen Hastings's ability to be effective. The Edwards family would have received hard services such as a homemaker or parent aide in addition to Helen Benedick's family counseling and parenting sessions. The counseling sessions themselves would have been longer and more frequent—perhaps more than once a week, but certainly more than once a month. Finally, intensive family preservation services would have had a mandate to set a deadline for a final decision about Marie.[5]

There are, however, cases of families who received intensive family preservation services and the end result is still a child fatality. The case of Eli Creekmore is one of the most widely publicized examples.[6]

Eli was a three-year-old boy who lived with his mother and father in Everett, Washington. He was kicked to death by his father in September 1986. Eli had been removed from his home on two occasions because of physical abuse, only to be returned home. Eli's maternal grandmother pleaded with caseworkers, only to be rebuffed as a meddling relative who seemed to have a grudge against her son-in-law.

Eli had initially come to the attention of Washington State's Child Protective Services (CPS) after his grandmother had reported he had been severely beaten by his father. The boy was initially removed from his home and then returned. Homebuilders became involved with the case and provided in-home services for four weeks. As the journalist Richard Wexler observed later, those were probably the safest four weeks of Eli's tragically short life.[7] While this statement may border on hyperbole—Wexler is a supporter of Homebuilders—Eli was not injured during those four weeks. The boy's safety could have been due to the Homebuilders services, due to the fact that he was so closely monitored, or simply due to the fact that most child abusers do not abuse their children every day, or even every week.

At the end of the four weeks, Homebuilders sent a letter to CPS warning them to be extra careful monitoring the Creekmore family and to remove Eli from the home if any further abuse occurred.[8]

Within a month after the Homebuilders intervention, Eli had been badly abused again. His grandmother and aunt took photos showing the bruises all over his face. When his grandmother and aunt took Eli out for ice cream, his mouth was so bloody and sore inside, he could not put the spoon in his mouth. Eli was treated at a local hospital, placed again with a foster family, and soon returned home yet again. A short time later, he was kicked to death by his father.

According to Richard Wexler, the Homebuilders intervention satisfied the requirement that Child Protective Services make "reasonable efforts," and that when Eli was abused again, CPS should have placed him in foster care and sought a termination of the Creekmores' parental rights. That this was not done, Wexler argues, was a function of overwork and/or incompetence at CPS.[9]

But overwork and incompetence at CPS were not to blame. Eli died because CPS does not have a "one strike and you're out" policy. Rather, CPS assumes that family preservation programs, if properly used, will work to protect children. Although CPS administrators and child welfare authorities do acknowledge that family preservation programs are not for everyone, they generally apply them to most families they serve, even if clear signs of danger to the child exist, as in the case of Eli Creekmore.

Do Family Preservation
Programs Work?

Of course, the question of whether intensive family preservation programs "work" cannot and should not be answered on the basis of a single case.

Joan Barthel, a freelance writer, wrote *For Children's Sake: The Promise of Family Preservation* for the Edna McConnell Clark Foundation. The book is full of glowing reports of how well family preservation works and how minimal the risks are. For example, Susan Kelley, director of the Division of Family Preservation Services, Office of Children and Youth Services, State of Michigan, testified that of 2,505 families who participated in intensive family preservation in Michigan in the first twelve months of the program, only one incident of abuse was reported.[10]

Barthel states, citing information provided by states that use intensive family preservation programs, that there is a documented 80 percent success rate in keeping families together one year after the intervention has ended. She also points out that evaluating family preservation programs is a complex task and that "there is not yet proof—using an academically acceptable, experimental design—that family preservation can decrease the number of placements in a state, and therefore save funds that would have otherwise have been spent on out-of-home care."[11]

An extensive review of evaluations of intensive family preservation programs found no evidence, based on methodologically acceptable research studies, that intensive family preservation programs were effective in reducing placements.[12]

But reducing placements should not be the measure of success. The main outcome variable should be *child safety*. The questions that must be asked when evaluating family preservation programs are: (1) Are children better protected? and (2) Are physical health, psychological health, and optimal development better for children who are served by family preservation programs? It is nearly criminal that these two questions have not been the focal points of evaluations of family preservation programs.

A two-year study of the Illinois Family First Program did look at these outcomes and found no differences in the number of subsequent confirmed reports of child abuse between the experimental groups that received intensive family preservation efforts and the control groups that received standard child welfare interventions.[13] Thus this study offers no evidence that family preservation programs reduce the risk of child abuse.

This discussion would remain merely an academic debate had family preservation programs remained simply one of many alternative interventions available to child welfare agencies. But by the 1990s, states and the federal government were, in the words of one sociologist, "running pell-mell into family preservation without fully considering the evidence for it."[14] The Omnibus Budget Reconciliation Act passed by Congress in August 1993 included the Family Preservation and Child Protection Reform Act (Senate S.596). This amendment to Title IV of the Social Security Act included a provision of

$1 billion over a five-year period to support state efforts at family preservation. Thus rather than being one approach, family preservation has become *the* approach, or at least the best funded and mostly widely touted one, in child welfare.

Abundant anecdotal accounts support the claim that intensive family preservation programs work, sometimes, for some families. Unfortunately, research has not yet been conducted that explains under what conditions they work and for which families they are most appropriate. I would argue that family preservation programs will probably never be effective for parents who are precontemplative—that is, who have seriously injured their children and are not ready for or interested in changing. The fact that both Darlene and Donald Edwards denied abusing Marie is a fairly concrete sign that they were precontemplative and that any form of action-oriented intervention, such as family preservation, was not going to be effective.

Figure 5.1 presents the two dimensions of risk that were discussed in chapter 3. Intensive family preservation programs would be most appropriate for families who fit the lower right cell—those where the level of risk is low and the stage of change is either action or maintenance. Family preservation could be used only with close monitoring for higher-risk families, but only those who are in either action or maintenance stages of change. Family preservation is clearly inappropriate for families who are precontemplative, contemplative, or in the preparation stage of change. On a day-to-day basis, workers still play Russian roulette with the lives of children, uncritically applying family preservation interventions

Figure 5.1
Two Dimensions of Risk Assessment
for Child Abuse and Neglect

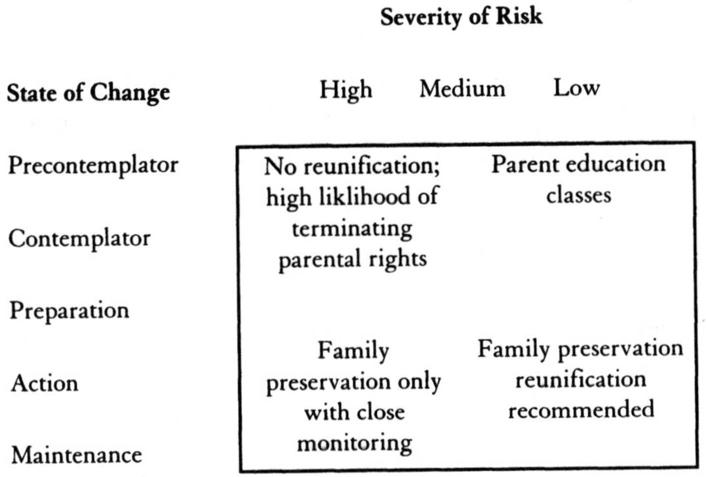

Severity of Risk

State of Change	High	Medium	Low
Precontemplator	No reunification; high liklihood of terminating parental rights		Parent education classes
Contemplator			
Preparation			
Action	Family preservation only with close monitoring		Family preservation reunification recommended
Maintenance			

until some glaring sign that a child is at risk emerges—and often well beyond that point.

Why is the child welfare system so "family focused" and not "child focused"?

THE HARSH 1980s

Nineteen-eighty ushered in not only a new national child welfare policy, as laid out in the Adoption Assistance and Child Welfare Act, but a new president and harsher social policies. The Reagan administration argued that programs for the poor had not simply failed, they had made the problems worse. A concentrated effort at the federal and state levels was made to reduce government spending for social programs. In the first few years of the Reagan administration, eligibility standards for Aid to Families with Dependent Children were raised, removing nearly half a million families from the welfare rolls and reducing benefits to hundreds of thousands more. A million people were cut from the food stamp program. The Comprehensive Employment and Training Act (CETA) was abandoned in 1982. Rules for unemployment insurance were tightened. Between 1982 and 1984 a million cases were reviewed and half were eliminated from the rolls of Social Security disability insurance. In 1982 nearly all the agencies in the Department of Health and Human Services suffered a 30 percent cut in personnel and budget.

The Impact on State, Local, and Private Agencies

As the doors of access to general social welfare slammed shut, families and children were channeled into the few remaining portals of the social welfare system. The child welfare system, and child protection system in particular, always had an open door because of mandatory reporting of child abuse and neglect. Some families arrived at the door because the lack of social and economic resources led them to abuse their children. Other families arrived because what would have been labeled "poverty" in the 1960s or even 1970s was being labeled "neglect" in the 1980s and 1990s.

The number of children in foster care seemed to decline in the early 1980s, probably as a result of the Adoption Assistance and Child Welfare Act and the policy of "reasonable efforts." But then the number began to increase. In 1982 slightly more than 250,000 children were in foster care. This number rose to 270,000 by 1985. From 1986 to 1990 the number of children in foster rose 45.4 percent and at the end of 1993 there were 464,000 children in foster care.[15] One estimate put the annual cost of foster care at $10 billion.[16]

It was clear to many professionals and policymakers that foster care had become an expensive "ambulance at the bottom of the cliff." Child welfare administrators, advocates, and some politicians agreed that there had to be a better way to spend $10 billion each year.

The unintended results of the war on the war on poverty was that child welfare agencies were receiving more and more reports of abuse and were having to service more and more families. At the same time, they were under the mandate of making "reasonable efforts."

If the child welfare community recognized the impact of the shift of federal and state policy, they did not protest. They may not have recognized the shift, since most of those in the system assumed that increased reporting meant more people were actually maltreating their children or that increased reporting was a function of increased public awareness. In fact, some administrators may have actually embraced the new caseload, since it was a mechanism to help families cut off from services from other programs. Furthermore, more cases justified more state and local budget support. Whether recognized or not, the child welfare caseload rose, funding rose (or at least was not cut), and the number of employees in the system rose.

Of course, the funding never was sufficient to meet the needs of the expanding caseload, with its increasingly complex cases. The system began, in the 1980s, to service more and more multi-problem families, more drug and alcohol abusers, crack babies, fetal alcohol syndrome babies, and HIV-positive parents and children. The system became more and more desperate for funding as states began feeling the crunch of falling revenues due to the recession of the late 1980s and early 1990s. How could the growing numbers of abused children and the cost of foster care be managed? Where would the new funding come from? The answer, or at least a partial answer, would be funds for family support and family preservation. Family preservation programs were a new source of funds for an overburdened system. Here, I believe, is when and how the child welfare system changed from one that was child-focused to one that would be family-focused.

THE POLITICS OF FAMILY PRESERVATION/FAMILY REUNIFICATION

If there was a time for a program and a program for the times, it was family preservation and the 1980s. Family preservation appealed to a broad political spectrum. Conservatives supported it because it is consistent with supporting the sanctity of the family, limiting state intervention into the private sphere of family life. The key feature of intensive family preservation programs—limited and budgeted services—was also attractive to fiscal conservatives. Here was a program that would help preserve families *and* cut the rising costs of foster care, which not only failed to preserve families but was thought to be harmful to children.

Family preservation also appealed to liberals, who saw it as consistent with the tradition of a caring government that supports needy families and children.

The promise that family preservation would simultaneously save money, strengthen families, *and* protect children was immensely attractive to politicians of all political persuasions.

In a climate where spending for social problems was becoming more and more constrained while the demand for such programs was growing, a program that could be supported on both sides of the political aisle was an almost irresistible opportunity for social activists, child advocates, and service providers. Family preservation programs could, if properly marketed, become the new funding stream that could plug the gap between service needs and resources.

The Foundations and the Overselling of Family Preservation

Although state and local agencies and service providers believed in the need for and the effectiveness of family preservation programs, the expansion of the concept of family preservation and the growing support for the programs, culminating in the $1 billion commitment of federal funds in 1993, could not have been achieved without the support, financial and otherwise, of two large and influential foundations. The Edna McConnell Clark Foundation in New York

City and the Annie E. Casey Foundation, recently of Green-wich, Connecticut, and now located in Baltimore, played cru-cial roles in the selling, or overselling, of family preservation. Both foundations have large endowments, make substantial expenditures each year, and have long-standing commitments to programs for children and families. The Annie E. Casey Foundation, with assets of $1.1 billion, is the twentieth largest nonprofit grant-giving foundation in the United States. It also ranks twentieth in expenditures. The Edna McConnell Clark Foundation has assets totaling $485 million.

Both foundations marketed family preservation with a near-religious zeal and substantial financial support. They funded start-up and demonstration programs and then promoted them by claiming they proved that a substantial number of place-ments could be prevented at little risk to children and that chil-dren would benefit because family bonds would be maintained and strengthened.[17]

Between 1984 and 1994 the Clark Foundation spent an esti-mated $4 million a year relentlessly promoting family preser-vation.[18] It funded a 1992 Bill Moyers TV special on family preservation that presented a glowing view of the programs and their philosophy. Here, Moyers and Clark said, was the silver bullet that could protect children and support families. The Clark Foundation and the Casey Foundation became the official repositories of expertise and data on family preserva-tion. State, local, and federal agencies and officials (including presidential advisers), relied on the two foundations for their evaluation data in support of family preservation.

The foundations as well as other interested parties chose to filter out criticism and data that contradicted claims about the effectiveness of family preservation.

When the believers are foundations who can invest millions of dollars each year in touting the programs and when the critics are academics who merely publish their research results in scholarly journals, the outcome is entirely predictable. State and local agency heads, legislators and legislative aides, governors and presidential administrations were told about the unqualified successes of family preservation and the tremendous cost savings. The skeptics and critics were either unknown or cast as merely academic gadflies.

Advocates and Special Interests

Child advocacy groups also played a role in the selling of family preservation. The Children's Defense Fund (CDF) and its head, Marian Wright Edelman, have for years been among the most widely respected and articulate advocates for children, especially minority children and children who live in poverty. Yet, oddly, the Children's Defense Fund has conspicuously omitted mention of child abuse and neglect in public presentations and advocacy activities. There are a few plausible explanations: The CDF may subsume the problem of abuse under the larger and more pressing issue of poverty. Or the CDF may consciously choose to avoid the issue of child abuse for fear that simply acknowledging abuse and neglect in the minority and disadvantaged communities might transform the problem into something seen as unique to minorities and the poor. Whatever the reason, child abuse has not found a place high on the agenda of the CDF.

The Children's Defense Fund warmly embraced the concept of family preservation and helped advance the Family Preservation and Child Protection Reform Act of 1993. Here was a program that would provide substantial new funding for families and children; that the money provided in the legislation was virtually the *only* new money for social programs in the Omnibus Budget Reconciliation Act was certainly not lost on the CDF.[19] After the legislation was enacted in August, the Administration on Children, Youth and Families in the Department of Health and Human Services began in September and October 1993 to establish standards for state planning grants for family preservation and family support programs; funding for such planning efforts began in 1994. The first-year funding level was $60 million—with $2 million reserved for research, training, and technical assistance, $600,000 reserved for grants to Indian tribes, and the balance available for states to establish statewide plans for family support and family preservation. In 1995, federal funding for family preservation and family support programs rose to $150 million ($6 million was set aside for evaluation, research, and training and $1.5 million for grants to Indian tribes). Funding would have eventually peaked at $225 million each year, but in 1997 the funds are scheduled to be put into block grants.

The Changing Political Winds

The passage of the Family Preservation and Child Protection Reform Act was the high point in the efforts to sell family preservation. Those of us who doubted the effectiveness of family preservation programs and the wisdom of the federal government's pumping a billion dollars into an unproven approach (at the exclusion of other types of approaches) were few in number and totally unorganized.

The situation changed dramatically with the fall 1994 elections, which brought new Republican majorities to both the House and the Senate. Although at this writing it is difficult to know what the actual result of this power shift will be, there is a new skepticism in Washington about the effectiveness of family preservation.

One of the first and central items on the Republicans' "Contract with America" was the Personal Responsibility Act. Although the welfare reform and block grant provisions of the act received most of the media attention and public policy debate, this legislation also included some major proposals related to child welfare and family preservation. First, the legislation that passed the House in the first hundred days would repeal the Adoption Assistance and Child Welfare Act of 1980. Thus states would no longer have to show that they had made "reasonable efforts" at keeping abused children with, or reuniting them with, their birth families in order to qualify for federal funding for adoption and foster care. Second, the Personal Responsibility Act also would repeal the Family Preservation and Support Program and its $1 billion budget that was allocated under the Family Preservation and Child Protection Reform Act of 1993. These programs would be replaced with a program of block grants to the states. As of this writing, it appears that the "reasonable efforts" provision will remain, as will funding for foster care and adoption.

Funds for family preservation and support will be folded into block grants to the states.

Of course, the reaction from the child welfare and child advocacy community to the proposed repeal of these programs, the allocation of funds as block grants, and the reduction of federal support for welfare and child welfare programs was uniformly and loudly negative. Many child advocacy groups dubbed the "Contract with America" the "Contract on America's Children."

It is too early for either side of the debate to know what the actual consequences and impact of the Personal Responsibility Act might be. Although the act would change the provisions that led to states' embracing family preservation and family reunification policies, the act also fails to provide any means of holding the states accountable for their child welfare and child protection policies and practices. Instead of one misguided federal policy, we will have fifty states each developing its own policies and practices. Obviously, some states could implement child-centered child welfare programs. Just as obviously, other states will continue to practice family preservation.

A second significant concern about the repeal of programs and the allocation of money through block grants is that the amount of money allocated will be less than was previously spent for child protection and child welfare programs. Of course, the hope is that block grant allocations will allow states to reduce their bureaucracies and thus have more funds for direct services. I think this is a bit naive. It is just as likely that even though states will not have to submit grant proposals and mountains of paperwork to qualify for federal funding, they will *not* reduce staff. Direct services funding will be reduced. Any reduction in service funding for an already overburdened child welfare system is going to put children at further risk.

There have been other signs that the selling of family preservation had cooled off. In April 1995 the U.S. Advisory Board on Child Abuse and Neglect issued its report, *A Nation's Shame: Fatal Child Abuse and Neglect in the United States.*[20] Among its recommendations after a two-year study of fatal child abuse and neglect were that all family programs adopt child safety as a major priority; all relevant state and federal legislation explicitly identify child safety as a goal; until the completion of needed research on families most likely to be helped by family preservation services, states use guidelines focusing on safety and well-being of children in determining whether such services are an appropriate option for a specific family; expedited termination of parental rights be developed in every state. While the board stopped short of mandating child safety as *the* central goal of all state and local child protection policies and practices, it did recognize the drawbacks of an unqualified acceptance of the effectiveness of family preservation programs and policies.

Even one of the major foundations that funded family preservation programs has moved off into a new direction. The Edna McConnell Clark Foundation announced in November 1994 that, over the next eighteen months, it would be discontinuing its core support for family preservation services, claiming extraordinary accomplishments in the field of family preservation and announcing a new grant-making agenda.[21] What was different about this report was that the foundation acknowledged some of the problems and dangers inherent in family preservation and in relying on a single intervention, such as Homebuilders.

The changing political winds seem to point to a shift by the federal government and some state governments from unqualified support for family preservation/reunification. Sentiment for a child-centered child welfare system seems to be growing. Yet, political changes notwithstanding, two problems remain unresolved. First, there is much concern that new welfare reform and child welfare reform legislation will, to use a child abuse metaphor, "throw the baby out with the bathwater." Repealing the Adoption Assistance and Child Welfare Act, the Family Preservation and Support Program, and even the Child Abuse Prevention and Treatment Act might not directly endanger children, might restore child safety as the focus of the child welfare system, and might actually make more funding available for child welfare services. On the other hand, the specter of fifty separate state child welfare policies, with no federal guidance or restraint, does not comfort many people on either side of the child welfare debate. More important, the real possibility that children will suffer disproportionately from proposed federal spending cuts will make it nearly impossible for even the best state child welfare agency to assure child safety. Lastly, although the zealous selling of family preservation seems to have become more muted of late, the field of child welfare and child protection still includes those who believe that family preservation works and is the best and most effective service the child welfare field has available.

CREATING A SAFE WORLD

The goals of current family preservation and family reunification efforts are certainly worthy and well intended: keeping children safe and families together. But, as we have seen, these goals are not necessarily compatible.

Why can we not keep children safe *and* preserve families? Why are we not able to identify when children are at risk and therefore family preservation is not indicated? Because, even with the recent changes of opinion and proposed policy, the ideology of family preservation and family reunification has been oversold. All the caveats about safety and the inappropriateness of family preservation services in some instances notwithstanding, the fact remains that the zeal with which family preservation was sold has convinced many policymakers and service providers that it is the best way to resolve the problems plaguing the child welfare system.

Those at the top of the child welfare administrations realize they need to balance child safety and family preservation, and although attracted by the new funds for preservation programs, do believe that such a balance can be achieved. The overburdened and undertrained line workers are less able to achieve such a balance. Sold on the effectiveness of family preservation, working under the mandate of reunification, and not provided with a credible or useful set of rules on which to base decisions about when family preservation programs are applicable, these workers often go ahead and use family preservation services even when they believe they may entail risk to a child's safety.

Supporters of family preservation programs consistently argue that the safety of children is the first priority. In response to a *Newsweek* article critical of current child welfare practices that emphasize family reunification, Marcia Allen, executive director of the National Resource Center on Family-Based Services at the University of Iowa, wrote in a letter to the editor:

> The fundamental flaw in your article is its assumption that the child-welfare system preserves families at all costs. That is absurd! Federal law simply mandates that *reasonable* efforts be made to maintain children with their families when possible.... Well-run family preservation programs always consider the safety of the child a first priority.[22]

Allen is correct in principle, but she drastically underestimates the impact of the marketing of family preservation and the impact of the $1 billion in federal support. Child welfare workers *do* try to preserve families at all costs. States have been receiving more and more funding to do exactly that. Allen's letter implies between the lines that when children are inappropriately returned to their families and injured or killed, it is because of a family preservation program that is "not well-run." This is simply not true. Well-run family preservation programs still place children in harm's way because such programs have an unrealistic belief in their own effectiveness—an unrealistic belief that has been fed and continues to be fed by the overmarketing of family preservation.

Illinois and Michigan call their family preservation programs "Families First." This title, I believe, says a great deal about what the real priority and goal of family preservation program is: families. It is difficult, if not nearly impossible, for state child welfare agencies to achieve the desired balance between child safety and family preservation. The family preservation programs themselves are not nearly as effective as the advocates and foundations have touted them to be.

Family preservation programs have been touted as the most effective way of intervening in families whose children are most likely to be placed outside the home. These families, in which the abuse and neglect are severe and the children are young, are probably the *least likely* to respond to family preservation efforts. Families in which the main problem is neglect and the children are older and less vulnerable to severe injury or death may be more likely to respond to family preservation efforts.

The cases of David Edwards, Eli Creekmore, and many other children bear stark witness to the incompatibility of preservation/reunification and safety. Efforts to keep all families together no matter what their history do occur, compromising the safety of many children. David Edwards should not have been left with his parents—and this is not simply hindsight, because the risk to him was obvious. Eli Creekmore should never have been returned to a father who had already brutalized him.

The single most important change that must occur if children are to be kept out of harm's way is to reinvent the child welfare system so that it places *children first.*

6

Children First

THE CASE OF DAVID EDWARDS REVEALS WHY THE *SYSTEM*, not just individuals or departments, fails to keep children out of harm's way. The Edwards family is in many ways a typical illustration of the perils and problems child protection services face today. It is not an isolated case. The cases of the millions of children who are maltreated and the thousands who are killed each year share disturbing similarities. It is not merely poor casework, a poorly administered child welfare department, or both that are to blame. While the social workers who worked with the Edwards family may not have been the best trained or the most insightful, and while the state Department of Children and Their Families may have a long history of problems, the Edwards case is far more typical of how cases are handled in more states than the system's defenders want to believe or want the public to know.

Concern and outrage often quickly give way to numbness and pessimism. But is the pessimism warranted? In fact, despite daily tragedies in the child welfare system, there is evidence that the past thirty years have seen slow but consistent improvements in our ability to prevent and treat child abuse and neglect. There is reason to believe that society has implemented and can continue to implement programs, services, and changes that protect children. The challenge now is to move to the next level of change and programs that truly create a safe world for children.

Since the early 1960s there has been a widespread belief that the problem of child abuse and neglect has been increasing in epidemic proportions. Data collected by the American Association for Protecting Children (a division of the American Humane Association), support this belief: They show that for all forms of maltreatment, reporting increased by 225 percent between 1976 and 1987.[1] The National Center on Child Abuse and Neglect, an agency within the federal Department of Health and Human Services, stated that countable cases of child maltreatment increased by 51 percent between 1980 and 1986. There were significant increases in the incidence of physical and sexual abuse, with physical abuse increasing by 58 percent and sexual abuse more than tripling between 1980 and 1986.[2] The yearly surveys conducted by the National Committee to Prevent Child Abuse, a privately funded child advocacy group, also find that the number of reports has risen each year.[3]

These trends suggest that three decades of effort to prevent and treat child abuse has failed to stem a rising tide of abuse. However, official reports do not measure the actual incidence of maltreatment, they only measure the number of cases that come to public and professional attention. Thus increased reporting might be a cause for optimism, since it could indicate that public awareness campaigns and changing agency practices are motivating more people to try to help children. It may be that Americans are undergoing a "moral passage" whereby behavior that formerly was considered acceptable is now seen as abuse. People may be less willing to quietly watch children being hurt by parents and are more willing to intervene.

In fact, my colleague Murray Straus and I found that parent self-reports of very severe violence toward children actually *declined* 47 percent between 1976 and 1985.[4] Subsequent yearly national surveys from 1988 through 1995, conducted by the National Committee to Prevent Child Abuse, found that the rates of severe violence toward children either remained stable or declined slightly.[5] Of course, it is possible that the decrease in reported rates of violence toward children may reflect only a decreased willingness of parents to report hitting their children. Yet even this is an important moral passage if more and more Americans feel that hitting their children is so wrong that they are no longer willing to report this behavior to interviewers. I am sure, however, that at least part of the decrease is the result of a real decline in the use of violence toward children.

Although the rates of abusive violence toward children may have declined, there is no evidence that the rate of children killed by their parents has decreased in the last ten years. And of those children who are killed, 30 to 50 percent are killed *after* their families have come to the attention of the child welfare system for suspected abuse. The child welfare system is in precarious shape, overwhelmed by reports, underfunded, and operating under the contradictory mandate to protect and preserve. While progress has been made, the world is still not safe enough for children.

A New Child-Centered Policy

The essential first step in creating a safe world for children is to abandon the fantasy that child welfare agencies can balance the goals of protecting children and preserving families, adopting instead a child-centered policy of family services. This is not a new policy, but rather a return to the policy of the early 1960s that established child safety as the overriding goal of the child welfare system.

If we have learned anything in the past thirty years, it is that we cannot achieve the delicate balance between keeping abused children safe and keeping them with their parents. The data we have on child welfare interventions support a child-centered policy that aims at reducing the risk for children and matching interventions to their needs. More important, the interventions must be applied efficiently enough that children do not languish in administrative limbo while court cases drag on.

The most compelling argument for abandoning the uniform policy of family reunification and family preservation comes from the data on children killed by their parents. Research clearly reveals the damage done by rigidly following the family preservation model. As I have noted, 30 to 50 percent of the children killed by parents or caretakers are killed *after* they were identified by child welfare agencies, were involved in interventions, and were either left in their homes or returned home after a short-term placement.

A second argument in favor of a child-centered policy is the data that support the conclusion that children's optimal development is dependent not on living with their birth parents, but on enjoying a nurturant relationship with a caring adult.[6] More important, children need to form this attachment during a finite developmental period, somewhere between the ages of two and ten. The failure of current policies is that they often leave children in limbo during this developmental stage while so-called reasonable efforts are being made to rehabilitate parents with the goal of reunification. As Dr. Albert Solnit, senior research scientist at the Yale Child Study Center, states, in order for a child to reach his or her potential for a full healthy and productive development, the child needs to feel wanted and to be provided with continuous affection and safe care on a permanent basis.[7]

It is time to abandon the myth that "the best foster family is not as good as a marginal biological family." The ability to make a baby does not ensure that a couple have, or ever will have, the ability to be adequate parents. The policy of family reunification and family preservation fails because it assumes that *all* biological parents can become fit and acceptable parents if only appropriate and sufficient support is provided.

Could Darlene Edwards have been helped to become a caring parent? Did David die because caseworkers did not provide enough services to Darlene? If Eli Creekmore's father had received a few more weeks of in-home services, would Eli be alive today? No, no, and no. Both Darlene Edwards and Eli Creekmore's father had histories of abusive behavior. Both were in denial about their abusive behavior and neither gave any sign that they were amenable to change. With the risk of future abusive behavior high and the likelihood of change low, no amount of services would have protected David and Eli.

The reality of current child welfare policy is that the rights of parents are almost always given greater weight than the rights of children. When a case of child maltreatment is adjudicated, the child welfare department is represented by its own counsel, the parents typically have representation, even if it is court-appointed, and the child often has representation, either a guardian *ad litem* or a court-appointed special advocate (CASA). Thus in theory, the playing field in the courtroom is level. But in practice it is not. First, the policy of "reasonable efforts" tilts the balance in favor of the rights of the parents. Second, the widespread belief that family preservation policies actually work further tilts the balance in favor of the parents. Third, the legal representation of the child is often a fiction. The guardian *ad litem* does not necessarily have to have legal training, nor does the CASA. Even when the CASA is a trained attorney, his or her caseload may be so great that providing adequate legal representation for the child is impossible.

Finally, the simple fact is that the most vulnerable children are the least able to defend themselves. The children whose risk of serious injury and death are greatest are those under one year of age; children one to three years old are the next most likely to be killed or grievously injured. These victims are not able to report on how they were injured or whether they feel safe. The perpetrators, on the other hand, may be able to explain away the injuries or offer heartfelt promises that this was an isolated event and "it won't happen again." Many perpetrators have themselves been abused, have been part of the child welfare system, and may have been institutionalized in residential placement facilities, juvenile treatment or detention facilities, or prisons. These experiences help them provide social workers and investigators with the answers they want to hear.

An additional force that has tilted the balance away from child safety is the federal support for family preservation. The lure of the $1 billion provides a powerful incentive for child welfare workers and agencies to preserve the family unit at the expense of child safety. This problem already exists in many agencies and will no doubt worsen if the funding continues to dictate the programs.

REVAMPING THE CHILD WELFARE SYSTEM

Despite the apparent decline in the rate of violence toward children in the last ten years and the increase in funding for child welfare agencies and services, the child welfare system has significant problems, if not a full-blown crisis. In the fall of 1990, the U.S. Advisory Board on Child Abuse and Neglect declared that abuse and neglect in the United States represented "a national emergency." The board cited the sheer scope of the problem: "In spite of the nation's avowed aim of protecting children, each year *hundreds of thousands* of them are being starved and abandoned, burned or severely beaten, raped and sodomized, berated and belittled" (emphasis in the original).[8]

Second, "the *system* the nation has developed to respond to child abuse and neglect is *failing*. It is not a question of acute failure of a single element of the system; there is chronic and critical multiple organ failure" (emphasis in the original).[9] The board's dire conclusion was the child protection system in the United States is so inadequate that the safety of the nation's children cannot be assured.

As we have seen, the basic flaw of the child protection system is that it has two inherently contradictory goals: protecting children and preserving families. The second essential problem is that the system *was never* designed to deal with millions of reports and hundreds of thousands of cases of abuse and neglect. When Dr. C. Henry Kempe and his colleagues "rediscovered" child abuse in the early 1960s, they genuinely believed only a few hundred children in the whole nation were truly in need of state intervention.[10] As a result, the greatest effort in the first decade of reawakened interest in child abuse was to draft and then implement the mandatory reporting laws. By the mid-1960s, no more than 6,000 cases of child abuse were confirmed each year.[11] But the combination of mandatory reporting laws and public awareness campaigns, with their toll-free 800 numbers for reporting, dramatically swelled the caseloads of child welfare agencies.

The caseloads grew for two other reasons. First, as noted, the definition of abuse and neglect was expanded beyond Kempe and his colleagues' rather narrow clinical definition of the "battered-child syndrome." Second, the reduction of social programs in the 1980s transformed many families from welfare cases into child welfare cases.

In addition to a new child-centered policy, four other fundamental changes must be made if the child protection system is to attain any reasonable degree of effectiveness: (1) Eliminate provisions for mandatory reporting. (2) Refocus child protection services on the most injurious and harmful forms of maltreatment. (3) Separate the process of investigation from case management and service provision. (4) Improve the training of child welfare caseworkers.

Eliminate Mandatory Reporting

The notion of abandoning the three-decade-long commitment to mandatory reporting is only slightly less heretical than arguing that family preservation programs are ineffective or even dangerous for some children. Mandatory reporting is the cornerstone of child protection efforts in the United States. Yet in the last thirty years, the United States has remained one of the few nations that requires child maltreatment reporting from professionals and, in some states, from the public at large. Great Britain, for one example, has carefully studied mandatory reporting in the United States and decided to forgo it as a feature of its child protection system. Given that I explained in chapter 2 that the sentinels, or mandatory reporters, are perhaps the most effective component of the child welfare system, this recommendation is not only heretical, it seems inconsistent with my own analysis. Even though the sentinels are the most effective part of the system, the overall system of mandatory reporting has many limitations and its continued functioning stands in the way of needed changes in the entire system. The sentinels should remain, but the requirement that they *must* report should be abandoned.

The requirement of mandatory reporting fails in a number of ways. First, as noted by Eli Newberger, a pediatrician at Children's Hospital, Boston, and a leader in the field of child protection for nearly twenty-five years, those children and families who are reported are disproportionately lower-class and minority. This disproportionate reporting includes both justified and unjustified reports. Similarly, middle-class children are underreported.

Second, and most important, mandatory reporting has overwhelmed the child protection system to the point that it can barely conduct investigations and rarely deliver meaningful and effective services.

Finally, mandatory reporting assumes that professionals are unwilling to treat child abuse and neglect on their own or, if willing to provide treatment, are less capable at it than state workers. But many professionals are quite capable of providing appropriate intervention, either in the form of compassionate treatment or referral for criminal and control interventions. As things stand now, professionals themselves do not make direct referrals to criminal justice and control agencies. Mandatory reports go to the child welfare system, which is generally responsible for making criminal justice referrals. Thus, eliminating mandatory reporting could actually *increase* the involvement of the criminal justice system.

Mandatory-reporting laws offer the false hope that one state agency has the resources, staff, training, and ability to investigate and serve all reported cases of child maltreatment. Our thirty-year experiment with mandatory reporting has not yielded adequate evidence that it does, in fact, create a safer world for children.

Eliminating mandatory reporting could decrease the number of false or less significant reports of maltreated children child welfare agencies have to investigate. Furthermore, eliminating mandatory reporting would place a greater burden on community professionals not only to recognize maltreatment of children, but to do something about it. Community professionals would be empowered to identify and *intervene* in cases of maltreated children. Still, the system can only be made more effective if community professionals and child welfare caseworkers focus their energies on the most dangerous and harmful forms of maltreatment. As I say throughout this book, better risk assessment is an absolute requirement if the child welfare system is to protect children.

Redefine the Scope of What Is Considered Child Abuse

A second controversial proposal comes from the work of Douglas Besharov, the first director of the National Center on Child Abuse and Neglect, who, as noted in chapter 2, argues that child abuse is "overreported." In Besharov's words, abused and neglected children are dying because they are not being reported to authorities and because the wrong children are being reported.[12] Not only do professionals like Dr. Systram fail to report some serious cases, but many professionals and laypersons, because of vague definitions of child abuse and neglect, make reports that are found to be invalid upon investigation. Because scarce resources are spent investigating reports that ultimately cannot be proven valid, fewer are available for valid cases of child abuse and neglect.

I do not agree that every report that has not been found "valid" upon investigation is a "false report," as Besharov's argument implies. The initial reports on David Edwards were not "validated" by the Department of Children and Their Families investigator—yet David was at significant risk. However, I do agree that many reports of abuse and neglect are made that waste scarce time and resources. These reports occur because the definitions of abuse and neglect are vague and because reporting all children at risk as the way of protecting children has been oversold.

It is time for the federal and state governments to revise the definition of child abuse and neglect. Child protection agencies cannot, and should not, deal with problems children experience that are essentially a result of poverty. Child protection agencies should not investigate spankings or teach parents not to spank their children. Child protection agencies cannot, and should not, be the arbitrator of sex abuse allegations proffered by those involved in antagonistic divorce proceedings.

We need a new legal definition of what constitutes the most

significant risks to children and the specific harms we will protect children from. The definitions need to focus on life-threatening, enduring risks to children.

Separate Investigation from Case Management and Services

There are, the joke goes, three great lies. The first is, "Of course I'll respect you in the morning"; the second is, "The check is in the mail"; the third is, "I'm from the government and I'm here to help you." With every investigation and every visit, child welfare workers tell the family they are there to help them, but the reality is they are also there to investigate and observe, and possibly initiate legal action to remove the child from the parents. Indeed, "investigation" may be the only service child welfare agencies deliver consistently and uniformly. That the child welfare system is asked to both investigate families *and* help families is the enduring paradox of the system. The only feasible way of resolving it is to separate the functions of investigation from the other child welfare functions, and then limit the other functions to case management.

Child abuse investigations are not social work. Investigators should not delude themselves that they are there to "help" the family. Their job is to determine whether abuse or neglect has occurred, who the likely perpetrator is, and the level of risk to the children remaining in the home.

By the same token, public child welfare agencies are ill-suited to the task of delivering services for children and families. The task of public child welfare agencies, after they have adequately and accurately investigated reports of maltreatment, is to manage the case and work in the best interests of the child. The services provided should be contracted to community agencies who are closer to the families. It is not feasible to expect a public child welfare worker to try to provide services to keep a family together while simultaneously monitoring the family for further abuse.

Training

If the current child welfare system is to be improved it will require three things: (1) training, (2) training, and (3) training. It is only a mild exaggeration to state that the system as it stands depends on poorly paid twenty-three-year-olds who majored in art history to make life-and-death decisions about child safety.

It is time for schools of social work to develop preprofessional tracks for students who intend to work in the child welfare system. The training should focus on risk assessment, investigation, case management, and current theory and research on child abuse.

Child welfare agencies must make a much greater commitment to training workers before giving them a full caseload. Child protection workers—both investigators and family service workers—who worked with the Edwards family had only twenty hours of training each before they assumed full caseloads. A great portion of the training was devoted to the department's rules and procedures and how to complete the myriad forms the department used. Even twenty hours of training that specifically focused on child welfare issues would be insufficient to prepare the average worker to assume a full caseload.

In addition, in-service training needs to be expanded. What was thought to be accurate information about causes, consequences, and correlates of child maltreatment ten years ago has changed greatly. Furthermore, child welfare workers need to expand and refine their knowledge and understanding of child development and family functioning.

Physicians, nurses, lawyers, and teachers are required to continue their professional educations; so should child welfare workers.

THE LEGAL SYSTEM

When a child who is known to the child welfare system is killed, such as David Edwards, Eli Creekmore, or Lisa Steinberg, one of the immediate reactions is to seek legislation that could prevent similar tragedies. There is a general feeling that the legal system is the best line of protection for children.

In the 1990s, the major types of legislation that could and should be enacted on behalf of children have been. In fact, we probably need to review old legislation rather than invest a great deal of time in new legislation. Legislation requiring mandatory reporting should be reconsidered, and probably rescinded in favor of a more effective system of identifying and servicing maltreated children. The legal definitions of child abuse need to be refocused so that the children at risk of greatest harm are identified and helped by the child welfare system. The social welfare system should help families where the overriding problems are those of poverty rather than inflicted injury or sexual abuse.

If the federal or state government is going to continue to mandate "reasonable efforts" to reunite families, then the federal legislation and the rules of implementation should specifically define what is meant by "reasonable efforts." Without a specific definition, the concept of "reasonable efforts" remains a Rorschach inkblot, variously interpreted by workers, agencies, and judges.

Beyond these changes, changes to existing legislation can help to refine child welfare practice and procedure. In the wake of the death of David Edwards, the legislature in his home state enacted a law that focused on the implementation of the "reasonable efforts" doctrine, adding two components to the statute related to the termination of parental rights. First, the law created a twelve-month time line for reunification. When a child is placed in state custody and the parent has a chronic substance abuse problem and the parent's prognosis indicates that the child will not be able to come home in a reasonable time, the state can move to terminate parental rights. The fact that a parent has been unable to provide care for a child for a period of twelve months due to substance abuse will constitute prima facie evidence of chronic substance abuse and an indicator that the parent will be unable to care for the child in the home within a reasonable time. (This particular law was enacted as a result of the Edwards case, but it would not have protected David, as neither of his parents had chronic substance abuse problems. However, Department of Children and Their Families administrators and caseworkers estimate that between 40 and 60 percent of their caseloads do involve caretakers with chronic or serious substance abuse problems.)

The second provision states that if a child has been placed in the custody of the Department of Children and Their Families and the court has previously terminated parental rights to another child from the same family, and the parent continues to lack the ability or willingness to respond to rehabilitative services, the court may terminate the parent's rights to all other children without having to enter into the process of reasonable efforts to reunite.[13] Here too, although the law was enacted as a result of the Edwards case, the law would only have protected David if the investigator had sought legal and/or physical custody of David from the Family Court. This is a good insight into the fact that a law is only as effective as the casework carried out by child welfare departments.

This particular law recognizes that it is not in the best interests of children to have them languish in foster care or another out-of-home placement while a parent goes through the long and often unsuccessful process of substance abuse treatment. The law also eliminates the dangerous and often deadly game of Russian roulette whereby the child welfare agency makes "reasonable efforts" at reunification for each child, even if parents have had their rights previously terminated for other children in the same household.

The major legal changes that need to be made are those that establish, formally and legally, the child-centered policy that will serve as the framework for public child welfare agencies and provide those agencies with appropriate and precise definitions of abuse and neglect, reasonable efforts, and specific timelines for services and decision making.

PLACEMENTS

The clear implication of a child-centered policy is that more, not fewer, terminations of parent rights will take place, and more, not fewer, children will need some kind of permanent placement. Where will all the children who need protection be placed?

The foster care system is already plagued by problems—problems that more than fifteen years ago led to the Adoption Assistance and Child Welfare Act and the emphasis on "reasonable efforts." These problems include the substantial number of children who are already in foster care—estimated at more than half a million; the high cost of foster care; and the fact that in some cases, foster parents are actually more dangerous to the child than the biological parents are. The claim that children are *more* likely to be abused in foster homes than in their birth homes is not supported by empirical research, however.

If the foster care system cannot absorb more children, if the system makes tremendous demands on federal, state, and local resources, and if some children are actually abused and neglected in foster care, what are the alternatives?

One of the alternatives that began to be quietly discussed in the early 1990s was the dreaded "O" word: Orphanages. Actually, the "O" word itself was not mentioned in polite discussion about the problems with the child welfare system and foster care; rather, terms like "group care," "residential placement," and "congregate care facilities" were used. The "O" word came out of the closet in the fall of 1994, after the midterm elections, when Speaker of the House Newt Gingrich suggested that welfare reform include orphanages for children whose parents (mostly mothers) could not rid themselves of drug problems, find jobs, and get off the welfare rolls within two years.

Orphanages evoke images out of *Oliver Twist:* of long dark hallways, cavernous dormitories, gruel; of poor children either emotionally abandoned or physically and sexually victimized. Orphanages are believed to be harmful to children, and an undesirable placement for children at risk.

Although today's orphanages are still a far cry from the warm and nurturant Boys Town of movie fame, they are neither as physically or emotionally barren as depicted by Dickens. The word *orphanages* is even out of date, as there are few actual orphans who live in today's congregate care facilities. But residential or group placements are an expensive alternative to traditional welfare programs: they can cost $40,000 and $50,000 per child per year compared to $6,000 for supporting a child in a welfare family or $12,000 in foster care. But from the standpoint of both expense and child safety, orphanages like Boys Town in Nebraska or the Milton Hershey School in Pennsylvania are plausible and cost-effective placements for abused and battered children, although they are generally not appropriate for children under three years of age.

Orphanages, whatever their value or limitations, are not the best place to begin a discussion of where to place children at risk. The discussion needs to begin by throwing out all the assumptions (myths and accurate assumptions alike) about caseloads and placements, because these assumptions are based on our experience with the doctrine of reasonable efforts and family reunification.

In a child-centered child welfare system, children at risk would not remain in abusive homes for long periods of time, experiencing repeated physical and sexual abuse and having their emotional and physical development compromised. Nor would they languish in foster care while the doctrine of reasonable efforts was applied long beyond the point where it was clear that abusive parents were not going to change. Abused children would not go in and out of the revolving door of foster care and their biological homes.

The main goal of a child-centered system would be to act expeditiously so that children could develop a nurturing relationship with an adult during the critical period of their development. Under a child-centered system, the goal would be to terminate parental rights, when appropriate, quickly enough so that children were not permanently harmed, physically or psychologically, and were made available for adoption early enough in their lives to enhance the likelihood of being adopted. (Adoptive parents generally prefer babies to older children.)

The case of Marie Edwards illustrates how the placement

problem can be solved without further burdening the foster care system or having to build costly residential facilities. Marie was ultimately adopted by her foster parents. In fact, they were willing to adopt her early in her placement, even though they knew she was going to be permanently disabled. The adoption was delayed because the state insisted on pursuing "reasonable efforts" with Donald and Darlene. David would have been even more easily adoptable had he been removed from his biological parents soon after his birth.

Because the most injurious and deadly abuse is inflicted on infants and toddlers, a child-centered policy would make children available for adoption much earlier in their lives, before many had been badly hurt, and at a point when they are the most likely to be adopted (prior to their first birthdays).

Even if earlier termination of parental rights leads to more adoptable children, foster care will still be needed for children as a transitional placement, either prior to return to their biological caretakers or prior to their being adopted. But it is also important to point out that more people would probably offer to be foster parents if they did not fear the state would hastily or inappropriately remove children from them and return them to dangerous homes.

The question of what is the most appropriate temporary placement for children will have to be reconsidered. Under the provisions of the Adoption Assistance and Child Welfare Act, state departments of child welfare are required to place children in the "least restrictive" environment, which means with relatives. Not insignificantly, these placements are somewhat less expensive: state departments of child welfare are allowed to pay lower rates for kin placement than for non-kin foster care.[14] In some cases kin care is safe and helpful. For instance, Darlene Edwards's parents might well have made good caretakers for Marie and David, had Donald allowed it. However, kin placement can be dangerous. Although not all abusive adults were abused as children, the rate of intergenerational transmission is high enough (between 30 and 70 percent) to warrant extra care in using other family members as caregivers. In addition, even if the kin caregivers are not, and have not been, abusive, the kin relationship is fraught with potential stresses, conflicts, and problems. Kin caregivers, in addition to being responsible for the child, are also given a "policing function": they must see to it that the biological parents are kept away from the children except during approved visits. For many kin caregivers, this policing function is more than they are able to manage. It is not unusual for one or both of the biological parents to move in with the kin caregiver during the time the child is placed.

Finally, group homes are a necessary part of the child protection system. There will always be maltreated children who, because of their physical or psychological conditions or the lack of alternatives, will need this type of permanent placement. The small group-home setting like that of the real-life Boys Town does allow children to develop a bond with a nurturant adult. Many children have thrived as adults after spending their formative years in residential placements.

CARING AND SAFE COMMUNITIES

Child abuse and neglect are not simply family problems or problems that the child welfare system alone can resolve. They are inextricably linked to the problems of alcohol and drug abuse, unemployment and underemployment, teenage pregnancy, poverty, homelessness, and street violence. It is not possible for the child welfare system to ensure children's safety unless they are able to live in communities that are free from rampant and random violence.[15] A child-centered social policy that calls for "children first" cannot be limited to improving the child welfare system. It has to focus public resources on creating safe and caring communities for children. Safe streets and safe schools have to accompany safe homes.

Public policy, like too much of child welfare policy, often pays only lip service to children. Although the rate of poverty among the elderly has declined dramatically since 1966 and has risen only slightly for those between eighteen and sixty-four, it has steadily increased for children since the mid-1970s. There has yet to be a concentrated effort to reduce the rate of poverty for children.

The community where David Edwards lived provides a window into how social policy often fails to meet the needs of children. When I completed my work on the fatality review panel that investigated David's death and I began to think about using his case as the basis of this book, I decided one afternoon to drive to the home where he had died. I was shaken by the blight and violence that permeated the neighborhood where David and Marie might have grown up. The street was littered with abandoned cars and broken glass. Stores and markets were now boarded-up shells. In the many vacant houses in the neighborhood, hardly a window was intact. The neighborhood stood in the shadow of an old textile factory, long ago deserted, a victim of the global economy that moved jobs first to the South and then to Third World nations.

This was not a neighborhood where I felt safe even to get out of my car; yet this was the neighborhood where David and his sister might have grown up. On the same day I visited David's neighborhood, there was a shooting incident at the local high school that David might have attended, and another shooting at a nearby convenience store.

This neighborhood was not nearly as bad as many of the neighborhoods where children are maltreated. David and Marie's father had a job and their mother had worked before she became pregnant with Marie. This was not a welfare family, yet in terms of social policy, David Edwards's community suffered from not-so-benign neglect. At the time of David's death a new governor had been elected. During the campaign, he had pledged to bring new jobs to the state and improve the economy. The governor was generally true to his word. He initiated major construction projects, including a convention center/hotel complex in the capital city, a new airport, and an upscale urban shopping mall. He was also successful in attracting a few thousand new jobs by granting tax benefits to firms that moved to, or opened new facilities in, the state. At this writing, the convention center complex is complete, the airport construction is under way, and the shopping mall is in the works. Unemployment dropped a bit and the state's economic picture, while not rosy, is at least brighter than before.

When I revisited David Edwards's neighborhood, nothing had changed. The new construction was only minutes from the Edwardses' apartment, yet there was absolutely no sign that it had done anything to improve the community. A drug deal was in progress a block from where I parked, not a single basketball hoop could be found on the neighborhood playground, and, as was the case four years earlier, a shooting and a homicide took place in the neighborhood the day I drove through. The jewelry factory where David's father had worked closed a year after David's death.

Politicians might argue that public works projects and tax breaks, while not directly improving communities like the one in which David Edwards would have grown up, do indirectly improve the lives of the people like David Edwards and his family. A rising tide, they say, carries all boats.

Of course, this is a lie. The economic development programs I described benefited the banks who lent money, the construction companies who landed the contracts, and the few thousand construction workers who had jobs for a few years. There is precious little evidence of any kind of a so-called trickle down of the benefits.

While child abuse and neglect does indeed cut across all

social classes, it does not do so evenly. The most horrific and dangerous acts of maltreatment tend to cluster in the most blighted and disadvantaged communities. Thus if we are going to create a safe world for children, a child-centered policy must target social policy and social resources for the most dangerous and harmful communities.

Child advocates generally argue that although primary prevention programs have a high initial cost, they are cost-effective, because if they work, they reduce outlays later. For instance, the cost of placing a child in a congregate care facility is between $40,000 and $70,000 a year. Detention for violent juveniles can cost between $25,000 and $50,000 a year. Jack Westman, a child psychiatrist at the University of Wisconsin, estimates that the worst-case scenario of child abuse and neglect is a cost to society of nearly $2 million per child—including social services, criminal justice costs, child welfare costs, and incarceration for violent crime as a juvenile and adult.[16]

So the calculus seems to come out in favor of investing in prevention programs and in creating caring and safe communities. But, critics often argue, how do we know *these* programs will work? How do we know that better schools, improved job opportunities, and safer, cleaner neighborhoods will actually prevent child abuse? After all, advocates claimed that intensive family preservation programs worked.

But I have not argued that family preservation programs fail; rather, I argue that they work only for some families and children under certain conditions. Family preservation is not a general panacea, and neither is primary prevention. Children are still abused in caring communities, but at a much lower rate than in the kind of neighborhood where David Edwards lived.

We cannot assure policymakers that all programs will work or be as cost-effective as promised. Of course, the development projects that are proposed to improve city and state economies also do not work as advertised either. The convention center/hotel complex built a few miles from the Edwards apartment was supposed to be an economic pump that would pay for itself in just a few years. Well, the few years have gone by and the convention center is as abandoned on many days as the factory behind the Edwards apartment.

A society that can subsidize a convention center and hotel, airport, and shopping mall can subsidize the physical and emotional well-being of children. Not all programs will work and not every program is effective for every family and child. Yet this is an investment we must make, because the costs of not making it, the cost in dollars, suffering, and lives, is simply much too high to pay.

It is not a lack of necessary knowledge or resources that constrains our ability to prevent abuse before it occurs and intervene effectively after a child has been harmed. It is not a lack of laws. It is not entirely a lack of will to provide the services that enhance children's ability to reach their developmental potentials. It is a persistent unwillingness to put children *first*. Children must come first in social policies and the allocation of social resources, children must come first in the words and deeds of the agencies that are entrusted with protecting them. It is time to move beyond the lip service paid to children and to develop a social structure, from top to bottom, that guarantees their safety, both by supporting families so that abuse will not occur in the first place and by absolutely guaranteeing the future safety and developmental integrity of children who have been abused and neglected.

Notes

Chapter 1. A Dangerous World

1. The term "illegitimate child," so common in the nineteenth and twentieth centuries, has now almost disappeared from daily usage in the 1990s (Arlene Skolnick, *Embattled Paradise: The American Family in the Age of Uncertainty* [New York: Basic Books, 1991]). The tremendous increase in the number of unmarried mothers and the change in social attitudes toward and norms about women, mothers, and families account for the recent disappearance of this term.

2. Barbara Nelson, *Making an Issue of Child Abuse: Political Agenda Setting for Social Problems* (Chicago: University of Chicago Press, 1984), provides a rich account of Mary Ellen Wilson's case and the media coverage of it.

3. See Michael Robin, "Historical Introduction: Sheltering Arms: The Roots of Child Protection," in *Child Abuse,* ed. Eli H. Newberger (Boston: Little, Brown, 1982), 1–41, for a historically accurate recounting of the story of Mary Ellen Wilson.

4. For Mary Ellen's complete story, see Stephen Lazoritz, "What Happened to Mary Ellen?" *Child Abuse and Neglect: The International Journal* 14, no. 2 (1990): 143–49.

5. F. Jonker and P. Jonker-Bakker, "Experiences with Ritualistic Abuse: A Case Study from the Netherlands," *Child Abuse and Neglect: The International Journal* 15, no. 3 (1991): 191–96.

6. Walter C. Young, Robert G. Sachs, Bennett G. Braun, and Ruth T. Watkins, "Patients Reporting Ritual Abuse in Childhood: A Clinical Syndrome Report of 37 Cases," *Child Abuse and Neglect: The International Journal* 15, no. 3 (1991): 181–89.

7. Frank W. Putnam, "The Satanic Ritual Abuse Controversy," *Child Abuse and Neglect: The International Journal* 15, no. 3 (1991): 175–79.

8. Ibid., 177.

9. David G. Bromly, "The Satanic Cult Scare," *Society* (May/June 1991): 55–66.

10. Senate Committee of the Judiciary, Subcommittee on

Juvenile Justice, *Child Kidnapping: Hearing before the Committee on the Judiciary,* 98th Cong., 1st sess., 12 July 1983. See also Joel Best, *Threatened Children: Rhetoric and Concern about Child Victims* (Chicago: University of Chicago Press, 1990).

11. Best, *Threatened Children.*

12. Ibid., 55.

13. David Finkelhor, Linda Meyer Williams, and Nanci Burns, *Nursery Crimes: Sexual Abuse in Day Care Centers* (Newbury Park, Calif.: Sage Publications, 1988).

14. Richard Wexler, *Wounded Innocents: The Real Victims of the War Against Children* (Buffalo, N.Y.: Prometheus Press, 1990).

15. Finkelhor, Williams, and Burns, *Nursery Crimes.*

16. Ibid.

CHAPTER 2. SENTINELS: MONITORING CHILD SAFETY

1. The concept of sentinels who look after vulnerable children is not new. Six thousand years ago, children in Mesopotamia had a patron goddess to watch over them. Child protection laws were legislated as long ago as 450 B.C. (see Samuel A. Radbill, "A History of Child Abuse and Infanticide," in *The Battered Child,* 3rd ed., ed. R. Helfer and C. Kempe [Chicago: University of Chicago Press, 1980], 3–20). Recent efforts are built around a system of individual state departments of child protective

services. The central component of the system is the mandatory child abuse and neglect reporting laws, developed in the 1960s. The Children's Bureau, an agency of the federal government, with the assistance of physicians such as C. Henry Kempe, developed model child abuse reporting legislation and worked to motivate each of the fifty states to enact versions of the model legislation; by the end of the 1960s, each state had legislated a child abuse reporting law. These laws were expanded and modified over the succeeding decades. For a discussion of the development of child abuse reporting laws, see Barbara Nelson, *Making an Issue of Child Abuse: Political Agenda Setting for Social Problems* (Chicago: University of Chicago Press, 1984).

2. David Gil, *Violence Against Children: Physical Child Abuse in the United States* (Cambridge, Mass.: Harvard University Press, 1970), 93–94.

3. Henry Kempe and his colleagues used observations of mothers and fathers in the delivery room as a means of predicting which caretakers were at high risk of abusing their children. See Jane D. Gray, Christy A. Cutler, Janet G. Dean, and C. Henry Kempe, "Prediction and Prevention of Child Abuse and Neglect," *Child Abuse and Neglect: The International Journal* 1 (1977): 45–58.

4. Nelson, *Making an Issue,* 76, 79.

5. Gil, *Violence Against Children.*

6. Saad Nagi, "Child Abuse and Neglect Programs: A National Overview," *Children Today* 4 (May–June 1975): 13–17.

7. Vincent Fontana, *Somewhere a Child Is Crying: Maltreatment—Causes and Prevention* (New York: Macmillan, 1973).

8. Senate Commitee on Labor and Public Welfare, Subcommittee on Children and Youth, *Child Abuse Prevention Act: Hearings on S.1191,* 93rd Cong., 1st sess., 1973.

9. Saad Nagi, *Child Maltreatment in the United States: A Challenge to Social Institutions* (New York: Columbia University Press, 1977).

10. U.S. Department of Health and Human Services, National Center on Child Abuse and Neglect, *Child Maltreatment 1993: Reports from the States to the National Center on Child Abuse and Neglect* (Washington, D.C.: U.S. Government Printing Office, 1995).

11. Kenneth Burgdorf, *Recognition and Reporting of Child Maltreatment* (Rockville, Md.: Westat, 1980).

12. Gail L. Zellman, "Child Abuse Reporting and Failure to Report Among Mandated Reporters," *Journal of Interpersonal Violence* 5 (March 1990): 3–22. Idem, "Report Decision-Making Patterns Among Mandated Child Abuse Reporters," *Child Abuse and Neglect: The International Journal* 14, no. 3 (1990): 325–36.

13. *Substantiated* means that the allegation of maltreatment or risk of maltreatment is supported or founded on the basis of state law or policy. *Indicated* means that maltreatment cannot be substantiated, but there is reason to suspect that the child was maltreated or at risk of maltreatment. (U.S. Department of Health and Human Services, National Center on Child Abuse and Neglect, *Child Maltreatment 1993*, B-4, B-6.)

14. Douglas Besharov, "'Doing Something' About Child Abuse: The Need to Narrow the Grounds for State Intervention," *Harvard Journal of Law and Public Policy* 8 (1985): 539–45. Idem, "Unfounded Allegations—A New Child Abuse Problem," *Public Interest* (Spring 1986): 18–33. Idem, "Reducing Unfounded Reports," *Journal of Interpersonal Violence* 6 (March 1991): 112–15. Idem, "Overreporting and Underreporting Are Twin Problems," in *Current Controversies on Family Violence,* ed. Richard J. Gelles and Donileen Loseke (Newbury Park, Calif.: Sage Publications, 1993), 257–72.

15. Richard Wexler, "Invasion of the Child Savers," *The Progressive,* September 1985, 19–22. Idem, *Wounded Innocents: The Real Victims of the War Against Children* (Buffalo, N.Y.: Prometheus Press, 1991).

16. David Finkelhor, "Is Child Abuse Overreported?" *Public Welfare* 69 (1990): 23–29. Idem, "The Main Problem Is Still Underreporting, Not Overreporting," in *Current Controversies on Family Violence,* 273–87.

17. Douglas Besharov, *Recognizing Child Abuse: A Guide for the Concerned* (New York: Free Press, 1990).

18. C. Henry Kempe, Frederick N. Silverman, Brandt F. Steele, William Droegemueller, and Henry K. Silver, "The Battered-Child Syndrome," *Journal of the American Medical Association* 181 (1962): 17–24.

19. Department of Health and Human Services, National Center on Child Abuse and Neglect, *Child Maltreatment 1993,* 3–7.

CHAPTER 3. INVESTIGATION AND RISK ASSESSMENT

1. The terms *substantiated* and *founded* are used by child protection agencies for those reports that are determined upon investigation to be valid cases of child abuse. *Unsubstantiated* or *unfounded* reports are not necessarily false reports; rather, these reports are classified thus if the investigator cannot find sufficient evidence on which to base a "substantiated" or "founded" classification.

2. When a postmortem investigation was carried out after David's death, there still was no record of a "chipped" elbow. The only X-ray available from the November 1989 visit was on David's right arm, and that revealed no fracture or "chip."

3. This estimate is based on the National Center on Child Abuse and Neglect, *Study Findings: Study of National Incidence and Prevalence of Child Abuse and Neglect: 1988* (Washington, D.C.: U.S. Department of Health and Human Services, 1988), 3–10.

4. R. A. Keller, L. F. Cicchinnelli, and D. M. Gardner, *A Comparative Analysis of Risk Assessment Models: Phase I Report* (Denver, Colo.: Applied Research Associates, 1988).

5. S. Berkowitz, *Findings from the State Survey Component of the Study of High Risk Child Abuse and Neglect Groups* (Rockville, Md.: Westat, 1991).

6. Howard J. Doueck, Diana J. English, Diane DePanfilis, and Gerald T. Moote, "Decision-Making in Child Protec-

tive Services: A Comparison of Selected Risk-Assessment Systems," *Child Welfare* 72 (September–October 1993): 441–52.

7. See, for example, Jerry P. Flanzer, "Alcohol and Other Drugs Are Key Causal Agents of Violence," in *Current Controversies on Family Violence,* ed. Richard J. Gelles and Donileen Loseke (Newbury Park, Calif.: Sage Publications, 1993), 171–81; and Richard J. Gelles, "Alcohol and Other Drugs Are Associated with Violence—They Are Not the Cause," in ibid., 182–96.

8. See Rebecca L. Hegar, Susan J. Zuravin, and John G. Orme, "Can We Predict Severe Abuse?" *Violence Update* 4 (September 1993): 1ff.; Glenn D. Wolfner and Richard J. Gelles, "A Profile of Violence Toward Children: A National Study," *Child Abuse and Neglect: The International Journal* 17 (1993): 197–212.

9. See, for example, Richard J. Gelles and Murray A. Straus, *Intimate Violence: The Causes and Consequences of Abuse in the American Family* (New York: Simon & Schuster, 1988).

10. See Byron Egeland, "A History of Abuse Is a Major Risk Factor for Abusing the Next Generation," in *Current Controversies on Family Violence,* 197–208; Joan Kaufman and Edward Zigler, "The Intergenerational Transmission of Abuse Is Overstated," in ibid., 209–21.

11. See Samuel Radbill, "A History of Child Abuse and Infanticide," in *The Battered Child,* ed. Ray Helfer and C. Henry Kempe, 2nd ed. (Chicago: University of Chicago Press, 1974), 3–21.

12. Linda Gordon, *Heroes of Their Own Lives: The Politics and History of Family Violence* (New York: Viking, 1988).

13. Gelles, "Alcohol and Other Drugs Are Associated with Violence."

14. Glenda Kaufman Kantor and Murray A. Straus, "The Drunken Bum Theory of Wife Beating," *Social Problems* 34 (1987): 213–30.

15. David A. Wolfe, B. Edwards, I. Manion, and C. Koverola, "Early Interventions for Parents at Risk of Child Abuse and Neglect," *Journal of Consulting Psychology* 56 (1988): 40–47.

16. See, for example, Thomas H. Holmes and Richard H. Raye, "The Social Readjustment Scale," *Journal of Psychosomatic Research* 11 (1967): 213–18.

17. David Gil, *Violence Against Children: Physical Child Abuse in the United States* (Cambridge, Mass.: Harvard University Press, 1970).

18. Murray A. Straus, "A Sociological Perspective on the Causes of Family Violence," in *Violence and the Family*, ed. M. R. Green (Boulder, Colo.: Westview, 1980), 7–31.

19. Brandt F. Steele, "The Child Abuser," in *Violence: Perspectives on Murder and Aggression*, ed. Irwin L. Kutash, Samuel B. Kutash, Louis B. Schlesinger, and associates (San Francisco: Jossey-Bass, 1978), 285–300.

20. The National Center on Child Abuse and Neglect conducted two national surveys that examined recognized and reported cases of child abuse and neglect. See Kenneth Burgdorf, *Recognition and Reporting of Child Maltreatment* (Rockville, Md.: Westat, 1980); and National

Center on Child Abuse and Neglect, *Study Findings: Study of National Incidence and Prevalence of Child Abuse and Neglect: 1988* (Washington, D.C.: U.S. Department of Health and Human Services, 1988). The American Humane Association tabulated official reported cases of child abuse and neglect from 1976 to 1987. See American Association for Protecting Children, *Highlights of Official Child Neglect and Abuse Reporting, 1986* (Denver: American Humane Association, 1988). With my colleague Murray Straus, I conducted two national surveys of family violence, including a look at violence toward children. Our first survey, in 1976, interviewed a nationally representative sample of more than 2,100 families, and our second survey, conducted in 1985, interviewed a nationally representative sample of 6,002 individuals. See Murray A. Straus, Richard J. Gelles, and Suzanne K. Steinmetz, *Behind Closed Doors: Violence in the American Family* (New York: Anchor/Doubleday, 1980); and Richard J. Gelles and Murray A. Straus, *Intimate Violence* (New York: Simon & Schuster, 1988.) There were thousands more small studies with nonrepresentative samples.

21. Jay Belsky, "Etiology of Child Maltreatment: A Developmental-Ecological Approach," *Psychological Bulletin* 114 (1993): 413–34.

22. Richard J. Gelles and Ake Edfeldt, "Violence Towards Children in the United States and Sweden," *Child Abuse and Neglect: The International Journal* 10 (1986): 501–10.

23. Murray A. Straus, "State and Regional Differences in U.S. Infant Homicide Rates in Relation to Sociocultural

Characteristics of the States," *Behavioral Sciences and the Law* 5 (1987): 61–75.

24. James O. Prochaska and Carlo C. DiClemente, "Toward a More Integrative Model of Change," *Psychotherapy: Theory, Research and Practice* 19 (1982): 276–88; idem "Stages and Processes of Self-Change in Smoking: Toward an Integrative Model of Change," *Journal of Consulting and Clinical Psychology* 5 (1983): 390–95; *The Transtheoretical Approach: Crossing Traditional Boundaries of Change* (Homewood, Ill.: Dow Jones/Irwin, 1984); James O. Prochaska, Wayne F. Velicer, Joseph S. Rossi, M. G. Goldstein, B. H. Marcus, W. Rakowski, Christine Fiore, Lisa H. Harlow, Colleen A. Redding, D. Rosenbloom, and Susan R. Rossi, "Stages of Change and Decisional Balance for Twelve Problem Behaviors," *Health Psychology* 13 (1994): 39–46.

Chapter 4. Unreasonable Efforts

1. American Association for Protecting Children, *Highlights of Official Child Neglect and Abuse Reporting, 1987* (Denver: American Humane Association, 1989). A. Shyne and A. Schroeder, *National Study of Social Services to Children and Their Families* (Washington, D.C.: Department of Health, Education and Welfare, 1978).

2. Richard P. Barth, Mark Courtney, Jill Duerr Berrick, and Vicky Albert, *From Child Abuse to Permanency Planning: Child Welfare Services and Placements* (New York: Aldine de Gruyter, 1994), 6.

3. Child welfare and child protective services were housed within the Department of Social and Rehabilitative Services in the 1970s. After a series of child abuse fatalities, the state reorganized children's services and created the Department of Child and Their Families in 1979. In 1993, after another series of child fatalities, the department changed its name to the Department of Children, Youth and Families. Such reorganizations and name changes are common around the country.

4. Public Law 96-272, sec. 471 a. 15, p. 503.

5. See Joan Kaufman and Edward Zigler, "Do Abused Children Become Abusive Parents?" *American Journal of Orthopsychiatry* 57 (1987): 186–92.

CHAPTER 5. THE FAILURE OF FAMILY PRESERVATION

1. Although one could refer to any program that attempts to keep abused children with or return them to their birth families as a *family preservation* program, the term *family preservation* is now mostly used to refer to intensive programs such as Homebuilders. *Intensive* means that caseworkers typically see only two or three families at a time for just four to six weeks, and spend up to twenty hours a week with a family if necessary. In order to conform to the current use of the term *family preservation*, this chapter refers to the traditional efforts to preserve families as "family reunification."

2. Joan Barthel, *For Children's Sake: The Promise of Family Preservation* (New York: Edna McConnell Clark Foundation, 1991).

3. Ibid., 14.

4. Ibid.

5. The list of characteristics of intensive family preservation programs is adapted from Peter Forsythe, "Homebuilders and Family Preservation," *Child and Youth Services Review* 14, no. 1–2 (1992): 37–47.

6. David Davis, producer, *The Unquiet Death of Eli Creekmore* (Seattle, Wash.: KCTS-TV, 1988).

7. Richard Wexler, *Wounded Innocents: The Real Victims of the War Against Child Abuse* (Buffalo, N.Y.: Prometheus Press, 1990).

8. Ibid., 265.

9. Ibid.

10. Barthel, *For Children's Sake,* 19.

11. Ibid., 43.

12. Amy M. Heneghan, Sarah M. Horwitz, and John M. Leventhal, "Evaluating Intensive Family Preservation Programs: A Methodological Review," paper presented at the Ambulatory Pediatrics Association meeting, Seattle, May 1994.

13. John R. Schuerman, Tina L. Rzepnicki, and Julia H. Littell, *Putting Families First: An Experiment in Family Preservation* (New York: Aldine de Gruyter, 1994).

14. Peter Rossi, quoted in Heather Mac Donald, "The Ideology of 'Family Preservation,'" *Public Interest* 115 (Spring 1994): 53.

15. Toshio Tatara, "Analysis of Foster Care Exit Rates in Twelve States From FY 84–FY 90," paper presented at the Foster Care Roundtable, Boys Town, Nebraska, May 20–22, 1994.

16. Ibid.

17. *Keeping Families Together: Facts on Family Preservation Services* (New York: Edna McConnell Clark Foundation, 1990).

18. Heather Mac Donald, "The Ideology of 'Family Preservation,'" 45–60.

19. Another reason for the CDF's support might be the belief that family preservation programs would diminish the likelihood of minority children being inappropriately removed from parents suspected of child abuse and neglect. One actual event that supports this fear occurred in Alabama in the late 1970s, when child protection investigators removed a girl from her home because it was deemed a "depraved" environment. The so-called depraved environment was that the black mother was living with a white man.

20. U.S. Advisory Board on Child Abuse and Neglect, *A Nation's Shame: Fatal Child Abuse and Neglect in the United States, A Report of the U.S. Advisory Board on Child Abuse and Neglect* (Washington, D.C.: Department of Health and Human Services, Administration for Children and Families, 1995). The U.S. Advisory Board on Child Abuse and Neglect was established in 1988 under the provisions of the Child Abuse Prevention and Treatment Act. The board has fifteen members who are

appointed by the Secretary of Health and Human Services. Members represent a wide range of disciplines and experiences, including physicians, psychologists, attorneys, and representatives from various community and professional groups.

21. Edna McConnell Clark Foundation Program for Children, Strategy Statement, November 1994.

22. "Why Leave Children with Bad Parents?" *Newsweek*, April 25, 1994; Marcia Allen, letter to the editor, ibid., May 16, 1994.

CHAPTER 6. CHILDREN FIRST

1. American Association for Protecting Children, *Highlights of Official Child Neglect and Abuse Reporting, 1987* (Denver: American Humane Association, 1989).

2. Kenneth Burgdorf, *Recognition and Reporting of Child Maltreatment* (Rockville, Md.: Westat, 1980). National Center on Child Abuse and Neglect, *Study Findings: Study of National Incidence and Prevalence of Child Abuse and Neglect: 1988* (Washington, D.C.: U.S. Department of Health and Human Services, 1988).

3. Karen McCurdy and Deborah Daro, *Current Trends in Child Abuse Reporting and Fatalities: The Results of the 1993 Fifty-State Survey* (Chicago: National Committee to Prevent Child Abuse, 1994).

4. Murray A. Straus and Richard J. Gelles, "Societal Change and Change in Family Violence from 1975 to

1985 as Revealed in Two National Surveys," *Journal of Marriage and the Family* 48 (1986): 465–79.

5. Deborah Daro and Richard J. Gelles, "Public Attitudes and Behaviors with Respect to Child Abuse Prevention," *Journal of Interpersonal Violence* 7 (1992): 513–17.

6. Byron Egeland and M. F. Erickson, "Rising Above the Past: Strategies for Helping New Mothers Break the Cycle of Abuse and Neglect," *Zero to Three* 11, no. 2 (1991): 29–35. L. A. Sroufe, "Infant–Caregiver Attachment and Adaptation in the Preschool: The Roots of Competence and Maladaptation," in *Development of Cognition, Affect, and Social Relations,* ed. M. Perlmutter (Hillsdale, N.J.: Lawrence Erlbaum, 1983), 41–81.

7. Albert J. Solnit, testimony before the House Committee on Ways and Means, Subcommittee on Human Resources, *Hearing on Federal Adoption Policy,* May 10, 1995.

8. U.S. Advisory Board on Child Abuse and Neglect, *Child Abuse and Neglect: Critical First Steps in Response to a National Emergency* (Washington, D.C.: U.S. Government Printing Office, 1990), 2.

9. Ibid.

10. C. Henry Kempe, Frederick N. Silverman, Brandt F. Steele, William Droegemueller, and Henry K. Silver, "The Battered-Child Syndrome," *Journal of the American Medical Association* 181 (1962): 17–24.

11. David Gil, *Violence Against Children: Physical Child Abuse in the United States* (Cambridge, Mass.: Harvard University Press, 1970).

12. Douglas Besharov, *Recognizing Child Abuse: A Guide for the Concerned* (New York: Free Press, 1990), 7.

13. State of Rhode Island, 94-H 8625, Substitute A. An Act Relating to Domestic Relations—Adoption of Children, 1994.

14. Richard P. Barth, Mark Courtney, Jill Duerr Berrick, and Vicky Albert, *From Child Abuse to Permanency Planning: Child Welfare Services and Placements* (New York: Aldine de Gruyter, 1994), chap. 9.

15. This aspect of creating a safe world for children has been thoroughly discussed in my earlier writing (see, for example, Murray A. Straus, Richard J. Gelles, and Suzanne K. Steinmetz, *Behind Closed Doors: Violence in the American Family* [New York: Anchor, 1980]; Richard J. Gelles and Murray A. Straus, *Intimate Violence: The Causes and Consequences of Abuse in the American Family* [New York: Simon & Schuster, 1988]) and in the writings of others. Alex Kotlowitz, for instance, has brilliantly chronicled the lives of two boys growing up amid the violence and fear of a Chicago housing project in *There Are No Children Here: The Story of Two Boys Growing Up in the Other America* (New York: Anchor, 1991). William Julius Wilson has provided a penetrating sociological analysis of the poverty and violence of the inner-city underclass in *The Truly Disadvantaged: The Inner City, the Underclass, and Public Policy* (Chicago: University of Chicago Press, 1987). Finally, Christopher Jencks has written an unsentimental and careful examination of the

policy approaches to the problems of inner-city poverty and criminal violence that affect the lives of children: *Rethinking Social Policy: Race, Poverty, and the Underclass* (New York: HarperCollins, 1992).

16. Jack C. Westman, *Licensing Parents: Can We Prevent Child Abuse and Neglect?* (New York: Plenum, 1994).

Index

Index

American Humane Association, 35, 146

American Medical Association, 33–34, 44

Annie E. Casey Foundation, 134

Annie Hall (movie), 84

Anonymous calls, 33, 58, 64

Asphyxiation, 3–4. *See also* Suffocation

Assessment workers, 55–57

Barthel, Joan, 126

Bartleson, Jack, 122

Battered-child syndrome, 44, 153

"Battered-Child Syndrome, The" (Kempe), 44

"Battered women's defense," 12

Berge, Henry, 10–11

Besharov, Douglas, 41, 43, 45–46, 155–56

Best, Joel, 18

Birth, of a new baby, as a risk factor, 80

Block grants, to states, 137–39

Boys Town, 163, 166

Brasser, Florence, 13

Britain, 153

Bromly, David, 15

Bruises, 3, 28; false explanations for, 5–6, 7, 59, 62; observed in physical exams, 32–33; spacing and position of, 7

Buckey, Peggy McMartin, 19–21

Buckey, Raymond, 19–21

Burning Bed, The (movie), 11–12

California, 19–21

Cannibalism, 15

CANTS (Child Abuse and Neglect Tracking System), 3–5, 28, 55, 58–59; anonymous calls to, 33, 58, 64; and risk assessment, 50–51

Cardiac arrest, 3

CASA (court-appointed special advocate), 150

Catholics, 24

CDF (Children's Defense Fund), 135–36

Cerebral palsy, 106–7

CETA (Comprehensive Employment and Training Act), 130

Child abuse: definition of, 43–45, 155–57, 159–60; models of, 80–86; prior history of, 66, 71, 74, 76–77

Child Abuse Prevention and Treatment Act, 140

CPSIA information can be obtained at www.ICGtesting.com
Printed in the USA
LVOW09s2347170116

470436LV00001B/62/P